THE FRE
CHANNEL

THE FRENCH CHANNEL PORTS

A VISITOR'S GUIDE TO
Boulogne, Caen, Calais,
Cherbourg, Dieppe, Dunkirk,
Le Havre, Roscoff, St Malo
and their Environs

David Wickers
and
Charlotte Atkins

PAPERMAC

First published 1987 by
PAPERMAC
a division of Macmillan Publishers Limited
4 Little Essex Street London WC2R 3LF
and Basingstoke

Associated companies in Auckland, Delhi, Dublin, Gaborone, Hamburg, Harare, Hong Kong, Johannesburg, Kuala Lumpur, Lagos, Manzini, Melbourne, Mexico City, Nairobi, New York, Singapore and Tokyo

British Library Cataloguing in Publication Data
Wickers, David
The French Channel ports: a visitor's guide to Boulogne, Caen, Calais, Cherbourg, Dieppe, Dunkirk, Le Havre, Roscoff, St Malo and their environs.
1. Coasts —— France   2. France —— Description and travel —— Guide-books
I. Title   II. Atkins, Charlotte
914.4'204838   DC601.3

ISBN 0-333-44074-9

Typeset by Wyvern Typesetting Limited, Bristol
Printed by Redwood Burn Limited, Trowbridge

Contents

Note

Whilst every effort has been made to achieve accuracy, the nature of the material contained in this guide means that factual data may be subject to change. The publishers and authors accept no responsibility for any errors or omissions.

The authors would be pleased to receive any information, recommendations, etc., from readers.

Acknowledgements

The authors would like to acknowledge the help they received in writing this book from the following people:

Tourist boards: Pauline Hallam, Director of Public Relations, French Government Tourist Office; Michel Agodi, Dieppe; Josiane Ermel, Ille-et-Vilaine; Odile Hébert, Calvados; Mme Labeye, Le Havre; Daniel Lede; Boulogne; Annie Le Goff, Finistère; Jacques Leprieur, La Manche; Jean-Pierre Rihouey, Cherbourg; Geoffrey Treble, Calais; Jacqueline Tréca, Dunkirk; Elizabeth Waelens, Boulogne.

Ferry companies: Sarah Gibbins (Bishop Associates), Sally Line; Toby Oliver, Brittany Ferries; Nick Stevens, Sealink British Ferries; Jane Larkham (Charles Barker Lyons), Sealink Dieppe; Paul Ovington, Townsend Thoresen; Kate Burchill (Biss Lancaster), Hoverspeed.

Introduction

Less than 10,000 years ago, before the melting waters of the Ice Age raised the level of the sea and flooded the plain between us and them, you could have walked across to 'France'. When, in ten years or so from now, the Channel Tunnel becomes a reality, you may even be able to do the same again. But until then British visitors to northern France have to settle for a ferry ride.

The vast majority of people passing through the ports have traditionally looked upon these landfalls merely as gateways to more distant holiday goals in the rest of France and beyond. The only reason they went to, say, Calais – still by far the most heavily subscribed port – was simply because a convenient ferry berthed at its jetties. If they happened to live in Dorset they might have preferred to travel from Weymouth to Cherbourg, again not because they were interested in what Cherbourg had to offer, but the route made sense in the overall holiday logistics.

Some seven million British visitors now travel annually by ferry to the nine French Channel ports. Over the last few years two new breeds of Channel hoppers have begun to enjoy France just for its ports and their surrounding *environs*. First came the day-trip shoppers, their ranks swelling to the proportions of invading armies as word got round about the prices. And the quality.

Lots of day-trippers also make the short journey to enjoy a wonderful lunch and a fruity bottle of wine amongst the locals at a fraction of the price of a British equivalent (if there is such a thing) and generally soak up the Gallic airs. Just because their chosen patch of France lies on the northern, long-neglected coastline does not imply any compromise on atmosphere. To cite just one of a hundred examples, we would defy anyone to stand in Boulogne's place Godefroy de Bouillon, engulfed by the city's medieval ramparts, and dispute the fact that no matter how many hundreds of miles they may drive into the hinterland they would be hard pushed to find anywhere more French than the scene before them.

The second category of visitors that are hopping across the Channel in ever-increasing numbers are the short-break holidaymakers. Along with the demise of the traditional British seaside fortnight and the mass summer exodus to hot costas, the two- and three-day off-season mini-break is one of the most phenomenal developments in the travel industry. One ferry company alone calculates that the mini-market has tripled over the last five years.

Usually travelling by car, the short-break visitors go to France to eat well, shop wisely, enjoy the sights and generally wallow in the intrinsic joys of their chosen port. But, unlike the shoppers, they also venture beyond the city limits to explore the surrounding countryside and coastline. Pottering around at their own pace, meandering along the spider's web of lesser roads that link the country's rural hamlets, seaside resorts, fishing villages and hideaway *auberges* is one of the great pleasures of Channel hopping. And, of course, when it comes to the return leg of the journey, the car offers a great shopping plus – the boot can be loaded with as many bargains as the law will allow.

All nine French Channel ports – Boulogne, Caen, Calais, Cherbourg, Dieppe, Dunkirk, Le Havre, Roscoff and St Malo – have two things in common: they are at the welcome end of one or more of the ferry/hovercraft routes from Britain, and each one offers an unmistakable taste of France. But the similarities end here. Each town bears a highly individual stamp, with sharply contrasting personalities such as the harshly historic and tightly knit appearance of St Malo and the super-modernity and spaciousness of Le Havre. Such differences can mean taking a boat trip for lunch on the Ile de Batz at Roscoff, weaving between the jagged rocks that lie just above or below the sea while watching scores of terns plunge beneath the surface in search of their next meal, or paying homage to a king of England's tomb in his abbey at Caen. Roughly 1100 kilometres (700 miles) separate Dunkirk, the most easterly of the ports, from Roscoff in the west, a distance that encompasses family resorts and elegant promenades, salt-marshes and spectacular cliffs, dunes and busy estuaries, deserted beaches and seawater cures.

The ports offer access not only to far-away France but also to their own, frequently beautiful, environs. Although widely dismissed in the race to the south, the scenery of northern France is worth a lifetime of visits. After all, unless it had something special to offer, it would hardly have become, over the centuries, one of the most fought-over patches of countryside in the world.

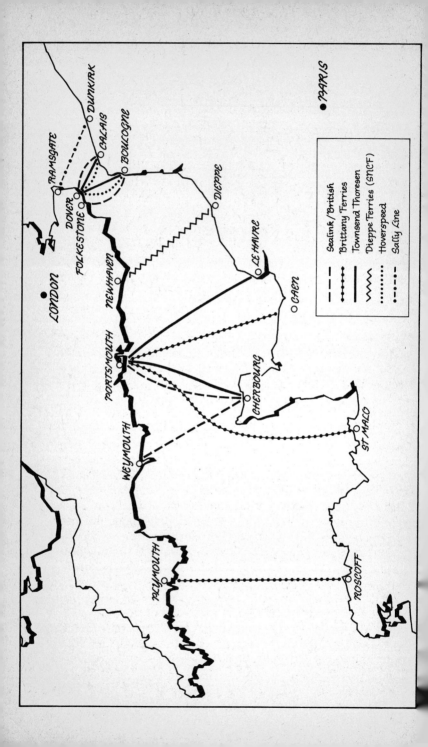

France for First Timers

Getting There

A motorist once telephoned the office of one of the ferry companies asking how much it would cost to take his car and caravan over the Channel. 'The price of the ticket depends on the number of metres' the booking clerk told the prospective traveller. 'I see,' said the caller. 'Well, could you tell me how many metres it is to France, then?'

The cost of crossing the Channel depends on a number of factors besides metres. Although fares on the shortest routes tend to be less, when balanced against the additional costs of getting there from your home town, other, longer routes, may well be economically more advantageous. Seven different companies operate fifteen cross-Channel routes to the nine French Channel ports, so be sure to consult the chart on p. 183 before deciding on the most convenient for you. The next step is to telephone the ferry operator that serves your chosen route (addresses on p. 184) or enquire at your nearest travel agent for information on sailings and fares.

Apart from day-trip return fares, which are always the cheapest, most of the ferry companies have special excursion fares which limit your stay on French soil to a maximum of either 60 or 120 hours. These excursion fares offer as much as a 50 per cent discount on the ordinary returns and are the obvious choice for the mini-break motorist. Fares also tend to be more expensive at weekends and during peak summer and bank holidays, so avoid them if you can. If this is impossible at least make sure you book well ahead to be sure of a place on the chosen sailing, especially if you are taking your car. Out of season it is possible to catch a ferry/hovercraft on the spur of the moment, turning up at the port an hour before the next sailing, especially if there are several daily sailings.

To make connections easier for the foot passenger in the Midlands and north-west England, British Rail have introduced direct trains to Folkestone, Dover and Newhaven which avoid the inconvenience of changing trains and stations in London. They have also reduced the minimum number of people travelling together to qualify for group travel rates to six passengers.

All-in Packages

All the ferry and hovercraft operators, as well as several specialist travel companies, now cater for the mini-break market by offering special all-in breaks that include not only the cross-Channel fare but also hotel accommodation either in the port itself or in the immediate vicinity. Amongst the most important tour operators are:

Argosy Holidays
Car Holidays Abroad
Eurobreaks
French Leave
Just Motoring
Paris Travel Service
The French Selection
Time Off
Winter Inn

In addition to these nationally established operators, several coach companies, especially those based in the south and south-east of England, will put together their own mini-break excursions to France. For details of these simply sift through the advertisements in your local newspaper or contact the individual coach companies listed in Yellow Pages.

Motoring

You need a full (not provisional) British driving licence, your car registration book (if you are not the legally registered owner you must carry a letter of authorisation from the owner of the vehicle, and hired vehicles need a hire car registration certificate VE103), and a GB plate (supplied when you buy your ticket, or at your departure port, by the ferry company or a motoring organisation). Minimum age for driving in France is eighteen years (sixteen for motorcycles not exceeding 80cc, eighteen if over 80cc).

For the novice motorist in France, driving on the 'wrong' side of the road will inevitably seem a terrifying prospect, a sure formula for pre-trip nightmares. But within minutes of leaving the ferry the *serrez à droite* technique will become second nature. First timers would be well advised to arrive during daylight hours, avoid the rush hour and, if possible, have a prior look at a map of the port (usually available from the ferry company). The biggest danger about driving on the right lies not in failing to cope but in losing concentration, especially after a stop for coffee or petrol. If the car or petrol station is on the 'other' side of the road be extra careful when resuming your journey.

The speed limits in France are as follows: 60 km/h in built-up areas (which begin at the town's entry sign); 90 km/h outside built-up areas; 110 km/h on dual-carriageways and toll-free motorways and 130 km/h on toll motorways/autoroutes. On wet roads lower speed limits are enforced. Visitors who have held a licence for less than a year must not exceed 90 km/h.

Most main roads in France now bear 'Passage Protégé' signs, meaning that traffic on that route has priority. In other cases, particularly on the smaller country lanes and in towns, traffic from the right has right of way.

Children under ten are not allowed to travel on the front seats of vehicles. Seat belts are compulsory as are hazard warning lights or the carrying of warning triangles. Visitors must carry a spare set of bulbs. It is not obligatory to fit amber headlight covers but lights must dip to the right and not dazzle oncoming vehicles. Motorcyclists must use headlights and wear crash helmets at all times.

All contraventions of the law may be punished by heavy, on-the-spot fines. (See also Insurance, below.)

If you don't have a vehicle and wish to travel within France you can find out about local bus services from tourist offices. Taxis are only allowed to be picked up from ranks – *stations de taxi*.

Parking

Parking can be a confusing experience for the first-time motorist in France. Most towns and city centres are classified as Blue Zones. You'll need to obtain and display on your windscreen a parking clock, set on the time you first arrive at the parking spot. These clocks are widely available from police stations, magazine kiosks and tobacconists. In many towns parking is also restricted to alternate sides of the road, often the odd-numbered side on odd days of the week and vice versa. In either situation look for the internationally understood road-signs before leaving your vehicle to the fate of the towaway truck.

Camping and Caravanning

Taking your own caravan to France is perfectly straightforward although the ferry/hovercraft fare will obviously be higher. Campsites throughout France are graded from one- to four-star and vary in price from around £6–£12 per day for a family of four including car. For a list of campsites send a 22×11cm SAE to the Camping Department, French Government Tourist Office, 178 Piccadilly, London W1V 0AL. If you turn up in France 'on spec' with your caravan or tent you can get information on the most convenient site to your port of call from the local tourist information office (Syndicat d'Initiative or Office de Tourisme), whose addresses you'll find in the individual chapters in this book. For caravanning in France you will need your caravan logbook and a complete inventory for customs clearance. Where a combined car plus caravan/trailer length is more than 7 metres, or weighs over 3500 kilograms, you must keep 15 metres clear of the vehicle in front of you when driving outside built-up areas.

Maps

Detailed plans of French towns are difficult to find in British bookshops but may be ordered – we recommend the Blay series (covering all the French Channel ports except Roscoff), which cost between £1.75 and £3.95 each. For road maps of each port's environs (within an approximate 50-kilometre radius) both Michelin and the Institut Géographique National (IGN) publish a comprehensive series. Michelin are scale 1:200,000 and cost £1.10; IGN Série Rouge are 1:250,000, Série Verte are 1:100,000 (and include long-distance footpaths), and both cost £2.95. All the above are available by mail order from Edward Stanford Ltd, International Map Centre, 12–14 Long Acre, London WC2E 9LP (☎ 01-836 1321).

Insurance

Holidaying abroad, for however short a time, is a risky business. All the St Christophers, rabbit paws and sprigs of lucky heather in the world won't guarantee your immunity from travel perils. What you can and should do is take out insurance so that if you do fall ill, have an accident, get your luggage stolen or suffer a car breakdown, the consequences won't be as financially devastating as they might have been. Non-existent or inadequate insurance cover can ruin far more than a holiday.

There are two types of insurance to consider. Personal travel insurance should cover unforeseeable illness, loss of luggage, personal liability, accident and cancellation. Membership of the EEC means that British visitors to France are entitled to a certain amount of free medical treatment. Form SA30, obtainable from the Department of Health and Social Security, gives full details of these rights and entitlements. Before you can obtain treatment in France you have to complete the application form CM1 and send it to your local DHSS office, who will supply you with a certificate of entitlement E111 – if you think these procedures cumbersome take out a basic holiday travel insurance instead, easily obtainable from a travel agent or an insurance broker.

Your car, or any other form of motorised transport, must be insured. Your UK insurance policy automatically gives you the legal minimum third party cover abroad but since this is only a *basic* cover you would be well advised to obtain an additional Green Card from your insurance company or broker which will guarantee the same cover as your domestic insurance policy.

According to a recent issue of *Holiday Which?* the British holidaymaker taking his car abroad runs a one in eleven chance of suffering a motor breakdown. Most of the problems are minor, fixed without too much trouble or cost, but if you are anxious about the consequences of a major breakdown or accident, perhaps necessitating the repatriation of the vehicle, the only real protection is an insurance policy through the AA, RAC, Caravan Club, Europ Assistance and other specialist brokers.

Phoning Home

Although the foreign telephone is usually given a wide berth it is actually far easier to use than you might imagine and today's direct-dial rates are a bargain, especially if you just want to pass on a message or check on the welfare of a friend or relative. If you are staying in a hotel, find out exactly how much they will charge to make such calls: although it may be more convenient to talk from your bedside you might find it's far cheaper to use the kiosk down the road. As in Britain, the telephone rates in France are cheaper in the evenings and at weekends.

To make an international call from a kiosk, lift the receiver and insert the coins (50-centime, 1-franc or 5-franc pieces) and dial 19 to connect you to the international network. Dial the country code (44 in the case of Britain) then your local STD area code BUT LEAVE OUT THE INITIAL ZERO. London, therefore, becomes 1 rather than 01. Then dial your number.

To dial France from Britain use the international access code – 010 – followed by the code for France – 33 – then the area code and the number.

Accommodation

If you are making your own arrangements and need hotel accommodation, you have two basic choices. Several French hotel chains have a central booking office in England, which you can either contact directly or through your travel agent. Amongst these are Climat de France (☎ 01-630 9161); France Accueil (☎ 0253 594185); Ibis (☎ 01-724 1000); Inter (☎ 01-938 2222) and Mapotel (☎ 01-940 9766).

If you want to book any of the hotels listed in this book you can either telephone and follow up with a letter of confirmation, or reserve by letter (make sure you have a reply before setting off). Most of them will be able to understand a simple letter in English – if you have any special requests (say, one cot, an adjacent room for Granny or a sea view) make sure the letter is in French. And if, once in France, you find you're going to be delayed, telephone ahead to ensure that the booking stays firm.

Hotels in France are officially categorised from one-star to four-star and four-star deluxe, and room rates are always displayed in each room, usually on the back of the door (along with emergency instructions in case of fire) and at the reception desk. Room prices within a hotel will also vary considerably, depending on the facilities (private bath, shower, toilet, etc.) and number of beds. Remember that the price is for the room, not the number of people in it. There are also 4000-odd Logis de France hotels: privately owned, family-run inns often located off the beaten track and offering excellent value for money. Some hotels described in this guide belong to the Relais du Silence group; they are always peacefully situated outside town and are similar to our country house hotels. French hotels are much cheaper than those in Britain and can be a little shabbier but you are paying for true Gallic atmosphere.

The price of a room in a French hotel does not usually include breakfast. The *petit déjeuner* usually costs about £1.50 and includes a pot of coffee or tea, freshly baked croissants, or freshly baked *baguettes*, butter and jam. No one in France will be surprised if you ask to see your room before taking it. And note that in addition to the bolster on the bed you will probably find pillows inside the wardrobe!

Hotels in the guide are categorised according to the price charged for a double room. Inexpensive: less than 100F; moderate: 100–200F; expensive: more than 200F.

Restaurants

Eating out is one of the great pleasures of France. Each of the ports, together with its surrounding area, is oozing with gastronomic temptations. The safest way to dine out is to choose restaurants that the French are obviously enjoying; the simplest way to dine is to opt for a *prix fixe* menu posted in the restaurant window which will comprise three or four courses for a set price (usually to include service and tax but not wine). There will be three or four choices in each course and if your French is wobbly take a dictionary. The menu of the day – *le menu* – is usually the best value in smaller restaurants.

One point to bear in mind for those travelling to France on a morning ferry: by the time you have added the one-hour time difference, cleared customs and passports, parked the car and found a place to eat, you may find you are too late for lunch. French restaurants usually stop serving punctually at two o'clock and no amount of grovelling will move them to re-kindle the oven. It is also worth remembering that although you may not be a wine drinker the French restaurateurs profit more from their drinks mark-up than their food, and will not be too happy with your abstemious habits. The best-value wines will be the *réserve de la maison* or *cuvée patron*. If tipping is included the menu will clearly state *service compris*. If it doesn't, you will be expected to add 10–15 per cent.

Restaurants listed in this guide are categorised according to the price range of fixed-price menus. Inexpensive: less than 70F; moderate: 70–140F; expensive: more than 140F.

Shopping

Shops in France open from between 9 a.m. and 6.30–7 p.m. but may close between noon and 2 p.m., especially in smaller towns. Many also close all day Monday or at least in the morning, and though the French Channel ports are more flexible about their shopping hours because of their British customers, don't count on buying your French goodies on either Sunday or on Monday morning.

Banks are open from 9 a.m. to noon and 2–4 p.m. and are closed either on Saturdays or Mondays, and Sundays and public holidays. American Express, Carte Bleu (Visa/Barclaycard), Diners Club and Eurocard (Mastercharge/Access) are widely accepted in hotels and the better-quality restaurants, several petrol stations and shops, but rarely hypermarkets. Ask your bank about traveller's cheques and Eurocheques. In general it is better to change sterling into French francs before you go. Otherwise change sterling at banks rather than Bureaux de Change or hotels.

The speediest method of shopping is to head for the nearest hypermarket. These gigantic retail outlets are situated on the outskirts of town because of the enormous amount of space they command. They were originally built to cater for the shopper with a car who could park easily and find numerous shops and products under one roof, including food, household goods, hi-fi equipment, fridge-freezers, gardening tools, clothes, furniture, a bank, a restaurant, a chemist, a hairdresser, a garage, etc., etc. Unprepossessing to look at, hypermarkets usually resemble corrugated iron, prefabricated factories, but inside they are ultra modern, clean and air-conditioned. They are well signposted from the nearest town centre, provide ample parking and are usually served by regular buses from the port. Most are open from Monday to Saturday (some close on Monday mornings) from 9 a.m. to 10 p.m. We found that a few now operate a trolley deposit scheme and ask for a 10-franc coin returnable when you return the trolley. Prices tend to be marginally cheaper than the stores in the town and although shopping in them is certainly convenient it is hard to beat the fun of pottering from *charcuterie* to *boulangerie* and on to the *épicerie* in the towns, let alone wandering around at the open stalls if your visit coincides with market day.

Some of the ports, notably Boulogne and Calais, have established Shopping Clubs whose members (shops, restaurants, car hire companies, etc.) agree to offer a special welcome to British visitors, as well as more tangible benefits such as discounts and trading stamps. Look for their window stickers.

For a guide to the best buys in France see below. For details of your customs and duty-free allowances see the chart on p. 187. For weights and measures – their metric equivalent – and Continental sizes see p. 189.

Note: Street numbers in the addresses for shops, hotels or restaurants are not included; they are very obscure in France and often don't exist on the actual building.

Department Stores

The following nationwide department stores have a branch in most of the French Channel ports:

Printemps: queen of French department stores. Similar to Debenhams, it often takes up a whole block and is easily recognisable by its canopies of pale green flowers on a white background. It is particularly good for clothes, kitchenware, jewellery, perfume and furniture. No food.

Nouvelles Galeries: for inexpensive, Marks and Spencer-type clothing, accessories, linen, perfumes, fashion, children's clothes and sporting goods. It often has a well-stocked supermarket, usually tucked away in the basement.

C & A: the same as in Britain, although clothes have more of a French flair about them.

Uniprix: like British Home Stores, but with a vast amount of space devoted to elegant displays of upmarket food, unusual varieties of cheeses, wines, vegetables, etc.

Prisunic: the nearest French equivalent to Woolworths, a 'food-to-footballs, frogs'-legs-to-*fines herbes*' emporium with something for everyone. Its huge stock of inexpensive novelties is popular with school children although few are particularly French in flavour. It often has a supermarket section.

Monoprix: very similar to Prisunic.

Best Buys

The following list is a guide to some of the best buys in France. It is not intended to be comprehensive since comparative prices, exchange rates and customs restrictions change and, besides, half the joy of shopping in France is to find your own bargains.

Food:
Olive, sunflower and walnut oil
Vinegar (cider and wine)
Coffee beans
Cheeses
Mustard
Sea salt
Bottled fruits and vegetables
Sweets, e.g., nougat from Montelimar, crystallised fruits from Provence, *marrons glacés*, home-made chocolates and truffles
Pastries (leave till the last minute and avoid fragile tins)
Jams
Tinned cassoulet
Fish soup

Drink:
Bottled beer
Wine
Perrier and other French mineral waters
French spirits and liqueurs (Pernod, Cointreau, etc.)

Household:
Glasses (especially Duralex)
Pans and casserole dishes (e.g., Le Creuset)
Bed linen
Kitchen knives
Electrical goods (coffee grinders, automatic filters, coffee machines, food processors, toasted sandwich makers, etc.)
Porcelain

General:
Children's clothes
Breton sweaters
Espadrilles
Folding BMX bicycles
DIY tools
Garden furniture and terracotta pots
Stationery
Perfume (even cheaper on the boat)
Knitting wool.

Buying alcohol

You'd be hard pushed to spot someone on a returning ferry who hadn't got a bag of clunking bottles at his feet or a crate or two stuffed in the car boot. But choose wisely, study the duty-free allowance table on page 187 and bear in mind the following:

The best savings to be made are on French-produced drinks such as Armagnac, Crème de Cassis and Calvados, and on cheap and cheerful table wines. Excise duty is currently 92p on a 75cl bottle and 85p on a 70cl bottle and this duty is the same regardless of bottle content, so the huge savings are to be made mainly at the bottom end of the price bracket. If you were to import twelve bottles of, say, Côtes du Rhône (the maximum allowance as long as they are bought in a French shop, duty paid), and assuming you don't bring any other alcohol into Britain, the saving on wine alone would work out at more than £10.

You *do* see the occasional foot passenger boarding with a building-site-type trolley loaded with crates of beer, but for most people the 50-litre upper allowance limit (roughly 88 pints) is far too heavy to carry. French beer comes in 12cl bottles that work out at around 17p each, usually packed in boxes of twelve. So take the car if you're buying in bulk.

Boulogne

Here, less than two hours from Folkestone, lies living proof that France really does begin just across the Channel. Boulogne is really a two-in-one town, an old and a new. Crowning a hilltop and easily spotted from the approaching ferry long before it pulls into the docks, stands the largely intact, medieval city, the Haute Ville. From within its thirteenth-century ramparts, Boulogne feels more like a small provincial town buried in the rural heartland of France than a swift ferry ride from the home shores. The old town comes complete with narrow, winding cobbled streets, a thirteenth-century belfry attached to an eighteenth-century town hall – one of the few redbrick buildings in town – a castle built in 1231 to defend the town walls from the threat of invaders, and a grand nineteenth-century cathedral built upon a Norman crypt.

Boulogne's Basse Ville, or new town, lies at the foot of the old, near the port. Largely rebuilt after its hefty damage from the allied bombs during the Second World War – 487 bombs landed here, destroying some 5000 buildings – its modern appearance will hardly deter the shoppers, winers and diners. The waterfront is home-base not only for the ferries but for hundreds of trawlers that make Boulogne the second largest fishing port in Europe; they unload some of the catch on the quai Gambetta. Docks and jetties aside, Boulogne also has a fine sandy beach, right beside the port and a popular haunt for windsurfers, and another at Le Portel, very safe and ideal for kids, near where the hovercraft docks.

Boulogne has been an important port since Roman times. In 55 BC Julius Caesar set out from here with 800 boats to conquer England. Modern-day Boulogne sits on the site of the flourishing Roman harbour, Gesoriacum, which later became Bononia. Centuries after Caesar, in 1544, Henry VIII hopped over from England and took Boulogne by siege, but he marched out six years later, finding it too difficult to defend, and the town was restored to France in 1550.

In 1803, a year after being proclaimed Emperor of France, Napoleon decided to follow the example of Julius Caesar. He was all set to invade, with his troops installed under canvas to the south of the port and an armada of 2000 flat-bottomed boats assembled in Boulogne's harbour, when Nelson destroyed the French fleet at Trafalgar and he abandoned his belligerent plans. Three kilometres north of town on the N1 is the Colonne de la Grande Armée, on which Napoleon broods, gazing away from England. In the museum you can see, amongst other things, his hat (but then there are lots of Napoleon's hats in lots of French museums). During the last war Hitler, like Napoleon, thought twice about attacking from Boulogne when he failed to gain air supremacy.

Do Not Miss

Whatever your mission in Boulogne, whether it's stocking up on wines and cheese or enjoying a gastronomic meal, save time for the uphill stroll from place Dalton to the **Haute Ville**. Even better, especially if you are well sated by that excessive lunch, take a brisk twenty-minute walk around the **ramparts**, pausing to look down from any of the four bow-fronted gateways or nineteen towers and to admire the horizon of the town's high-pitched rooftops or the views of the docks, or the distant surrounding forests. On the clearest of days you can just make out the coast of Britain.

At more or less every point along the walk you will be able to see the **Cathédrale Notre Dame**. After admiring its various exterior facets, including its magnificent Italianate dome, explore its interior with its priceless marble and mosaic altar, made in the Vatican workshop and brought to Boulogne in 1866 in nine chariots pulled by thirty horses. Other impressive features in the cathedral include its central soaring nave and thin fluted columns on either side, displaying a lightness of touch quite rare in a European town this far north, the statue of Notre Dame, made from a 1000-year-old cedar branch in Lebanon, and the crypt, a labyrinth of tiny passages, a vestige of the original Norman cathedral and the place where Edward II of England married Isabelle of France.

The **castle**, built in the thirteenth century on the foundation of the original Roman walls and strengthened by Louis XIV's military architect Vauban, can only be seen at close quarters from the ramparts, as it is currently closed for restoration work. When completed it will house the town's museum and, naturally, Napoleon's hat.

The **House of San Martin** in Grande Rue was the home of South America's great liberator after he was exiled from Peru in 1822 by Simon Bolivar. It is now a museum containing historic uniforms, his domestic quarters and an exhibition devoted to the history of Argentina.

Shopping Spree

The bargains to be had in Boulogne's boutiques, stores, shops, supermarkets, hypermarket and open market have helped to create an entirely new phenomenon in foreign travel. Last year nearly a million and a half people climbed aboard a ferry or hovercraft, armed with empty bags and shopping trolleys, and stormed the town's retail outlets like an invading army.

Virtually all the shops that lie within the medieval ramparts line the rue de Lille. 'Downtown', the most important shopping streets are the Grande Rue and rue Faidherbe, both one-way thoroughfares that link the port with the old town, and rues Thiers (where you'll find a high proportion of Boulogne's trendy clothes shops including Bus Stop, Benetton, Promod and Actuel), Victor Hugo and Nationale.

Vins de France/Coteaux de France: working your way up from the Place Godefroy de Bouillon in the old town, and yo-yo-ing back and forth across the relatively traffic-free rue de Lille, you'll come to two of Boulogne's excellent specialist wine stores, the Vins de

France and Cotaux de France (the latter open Sundays), both selling a range of expensive quality vintages as well as bargain special offers and a few groceries. *Rue de Lille*.

Sabine: a deceptively large and fascinating boutique selling interesting jewellery, Indian-style artisan clothes, hand-painted silk scarves, hand-smocked dresses, locally made crafts and so on; the room at the back is home to a small paintings and sculpture gallery, with exhibitions changing every two months or so. There's also a tiny tea-room. *Rue de Lille*.

Vanheekhoet: if you're looking for beautiful designs in kitchenware, this store has them all, including the best of floral pottery from nearby Desvres and other carefully selected ceramics, pretty pots, vases, glassware, pictures and a host of gift ideas. *Rue de Lille*.

Béthouart: this is a fine pâtisserie, *confiserie* and tea-shop combined, famed for its wonderful-looking and delicious-to-eat marzipan in the shape of fruit or fish. Their old-fashioned tins of Bêtises, mint-flavoured boiled sweets, also make attractive presents (and the tins have a thousand and one uses after the sweets have long gone). Béthouart also makes its own delicious ice-cream. The neon sign outside the *Salon du Thé* translates as 'all made with butter' – an indication of the quality of its cakes. *Rue de Lille*.

Philippe Olivier: a master cheesemaker whose *fromagerie* is almost a Boulogne institution. Apart from selling an enormous range of 200 cheeses, Philippe regularly supplies Harrods and several of London's top restaurants. If you can't make up your mind, opt for Camembert steeped in punchy Calvados or one of the local specialities like Maroilles, soft, slightly salty and gold; Mimolette, an orange-coloured cheese from Flanders; or St Paulin, delicious with Muscadet or Pinot Blanc. *Rue Thiers*.

Descamps: a branch of the stylish French chain that specialises in beautiful bed and bathroom linen in delicate colours and designs that you'll not find too easily in Britain (unless you visit their Sloane Street store in London, that is). *Rue Thiers*.

Nouvelles Galeries: the largest department store in Boulogne and a vital port of call for inexpensive Marks and Spencer-type goods: clothing, accessories, linens and perfume on the ground floor;

fashion and children's clothes and sporting goods on the first floor and an admirably stocked supermarket in the basement with many local specialities. The store stands a block deep so you can also approach it from rue Victor Hugo, which often tends to confuse British visitors who enter by one and leave by the other door (including people who wonder what happened to their spouses they left waiting outside). *Rue Thiers.*

Pâtisserie Moderne: *moderne* is the last way to describe this blissful pâtisserie with its art deco interior, complete with delicate neon lighting on the ceiling. It sells sandwiches, gâteaux, sweets, chocolate and, completely out of character, hot dogs (the sign actually reads 'hot dog's'. Hot dog's what? One may well ask). *Rue Faidherbe.*

Armand Thiery: a rather smart men's clothing store with styles to make all ages feel comfortable and a number of well-known labels sewn inside, including Rodier, Yves St Laurent, Guy Laroche and Pierre Cardin. *Rue Faidherbe.*

Brûlerie Faidherbe: a few discerning bottles of wine racked in old wooden boxes are squeezed amongst a selection of teas, home-roasted coffee and confectionery. Open most Sunday afternoons. *Rue Faidherbe.*

Monteil: an enormous milliners, an unusual sight for most British people, selling all sorts of hats from sombreros to Stetsons, sailors' to scouts' caps, bonnets and 'Boulogne je t'adore' sunhats. *Rue Faidherbe.*

Laines Berger du Nord: 'Wool of the shepherd of the north' sells both brightly designed sweaters as well as skeins of wool, with a high proportion of fluffy mohair and angora. *Rue Faidherbe.*

Caprice: a grand, very elegant store selling top-quality china, porcelain miniatures and glassware, cutlery, Limoges pottery and pewter ornaments. *Rue Nationale.*

Reflets de Paris: a rather chic women's clothing boutique with attractive blue window blinds and art nouveau lettering. The other boutique to investigate in this street is Cloé, again with fine designs at expensive prices. *Rue Nationale.*

Lacroix: upmarket clothes for upmarket men. *Grande Rue.*

Prisunic: you'll find a busy branch in *Grande Rue.*

Derrien: selling some of the tastiest *charcuterie* in town, including foie gras, stuffed snails, *boudin* sausage, pigs' trotters and quiches. *Grande Rue.*

Parfumerie Gilliocq: with its pink façade and delicate wrought-iron and glass canopy, this is undoubtedly one of the best places in town to buy the finer fragrances, including a wide range of men's toiletries as well as all the global names in women's perfume. *Grande Rue.*

Lugand Pâtisserie: 'caféteria, crêperie, pâtisserie, chocolatier', this is one of Boulogne's landmarks and an excellent place to rest your weary shopper's feet over a cup of tea or coffee and something delicious and fattening. Or you can take away some of its beautiful cakes – the fruit flans in particular are a work of art, or try some of the *marrons glacés* or any of the thirty kinds of home-made chocolates. *Grande Rue.*

Comtesse du Barry: Pascale and François Bravi's new shop is almost an art gallery of '*gastronomie des quatre saisons*. Their fine epicurean temptations include tins of pâtés, cassoulets and *gigot de poulet en gelée aux Sauternes*, delicate jams – such as rhubarb and banana or peach soufflé – boxes of Bordeaux wines and beautiful gift-packs for friends who have no waistline to worry about. *Grande Rue.*

Centre Commercial de la Liane: a collection of shops, a smaller version of the Auchan hypermarket, and more conveniently situated for those who come to Boulogne without a car (although there is an underground car park for those who do). It stands just behind the Hotel Ibis, only a few minutes' walk from the ferry terminal. The largest shop, and best known to British visitors, is the Champion supermarket (open from 9 a.m. to 8.30 p.m. daily except Sunday; closes 8 p.m. Saturdays). Here you can buy all your likely needs under one roof: there's an excellent delicatessen section, plus endless wines, shelves lined with cheeses, beer, spirits, kitchenware, fresh fruits and vegetables and most of the other French bargains you are likely to be looking for. Just opposite Champion is a specialist wine and cheese store called L'Flu à Jérôme, which sells the popular Nicolas wines and always has bin-loads of special *promotions,* usually handy triple-bottle packs at ridiculously low prices. There is also a very good cafeteria called Presto, low on atmosphere but also low on prices.

Le Chais: you don't have to drive all the way to the vineyards before buying wine from one of the bulk wholesale outlets. Le Chais is an enormous warehouse filled with around 200,000 bottles of wine (plus a range of spirits, beers and bottled waters) from all over the country. You simply grab one of the trolleys and 'self-drive' yourself up and down the racks, picking your way through the country's vineyards with prices ranging from less than 5 francs to well over a small fortune. You can also buy in bulk, in 4- and 10-litre *cubitaineurs,* for example, which you transfer to bottles once you get home. Le Chais is closed on Monday. *Rue des Deux Ponts* (on the outskirts of town – ask the tourist office to mark it on a map).

L'Auchan hypermarket: a whale of a store, or rather stores in addition to the main supermarket, where you'll find everything from deep-freezes to lawn mowers as well as an enormous range of food and wines. Outside, there's plenty of space to park your personal articulated truck. L'Auchan lies 8 kilometres outside town on the D940 road to St Omer and is open until 10 p.m. every day except Sunday. Buses to La Capelle operate at approximately hourly intervals from just outside the Centre Commercial.

Boulogne's market takes place every Wednesday and Saturday in the place Dalton, from seven in the morning till lunchtime. Set right in the heart of town around the old Church of Saint Nicolas, the market is an experience you shouldn't miss. Mainly devoted to food and general produce, it is a lively bustle of stalls and open-sided vans, many of which are owned and run by local farmers. The range of cheeses, pâtés, meats, fruit, vegetables and flowers they sell is both bewildering and mouth-watering. Even if you're not buying, the attractive presentation of the produce and the sparkling freshness of the vegetables makes the market a sightseeing trip in its own right. There are lots of surprises for the British browser, too, such as horse-meat, a prized delicacy in France, scores of live rabbits, calmly nibbling grass in their hutches, unaware that they are on offer at 30F a kilo, fresh herbs, goose eggs and caged chickens.

A Place to Stay

Boulogne offers a range of accommodation to suit all tastes and pockets but because of the town's popularity during the summer months it is always wise to book in advance.

De Lorraine: tucked away in a quiet corner of town this 25-year-old, two-star friendly hotel is owned and run by the Belgian-born Vanhasbroucks. There are twenty-one rooms but, sadly, it closes during the winter. *Pl. de Lorraine,* ☎ *21 31 34 78. Inexpensive to moderate.*

Des Arts: it seems a little shabby at the seams but several rooms enjoy one of the best views in town, overlooking the ferries shuffling up to or away from their berth. *Quai Gambetta,* ☎ *21 31 53 31. Inexpensive to moderate.*

De Londres: situated on the central bus parking area – not really an attractive prospect, but a convenient one if you don't have a car and want to visit the surrounding countryside and beaches. Cheerful rooms and a friendly welcome from Mme Quennehen. *Pl. de France,* ☎ *21 31 35 63. Moderate.*

Métropole: from the perspective of a comfy chair in the Métropole's back garden, surrounded by ivy-covered walls, a rockery and roses, you could be miles from the Boulogne bustle that lies outside the front door. Other pluses include colour TV tuned to all four British channels, fifty-seven all-mod-con rooms and a lift (there are five floors so it's an essential). *Rue Thiers,* ☎ *21 31 54 30. Moderate to expensive.*

Faidherbe: if someone says '*Bonjour, Général*' when you walk in it is not the reception clerk mistaking you for someone of high-ranking military honours but the pet parrot saying hello to himself. Général the parrot lives in a cage in the elegant, brassy foyer, warmed by a fire in winter. Located conveniently at the port end of town, this is a popular resting spot for British visitors. *Rue Faidherbe*, ☎ *21 31 60 93. Moderate to expensive.*

Alexandra: Bic razors individually wrapped and on sale at Reception are either a sign of Mme Youyou's caring approach to hostelry or her hatred of beards and hairy legs. Simple rooms, some with facilities, some without, and no restaurant, but the Youyous own L'Aquarium fish restaurant down the road and around the corner on rue Coquelin. *Rue Thiers*, ☎ *21 30 52 22. Inexpensive to moderate.*

Au Sleeping: this slickly modern hotel feels more like a dorm on a Scandinavian campus than a Gallic retreat but the clean lines and efficient management will appeal to travellers who don't attach any value to the Gallic style of fixtures and fittings. *Blvd Daunou*, ☎ *21 80 62 79. Expensive.*

And Somewhere to Eat

As soon as you step off the ferry a salty breeze slaps you on the cheek and you may well catch a whiff of herring in the tangy Channel air. In the Middle Ages Boulogne was rather unflatteringly referred to as *une ville harengère*, a herring town. Today, because it is France's largest fishing port, don't be surprised to find fish heavily featured on any menu, for starters and for main dishes. It's usually excellent, being so freshly caught, and there is a wide variety from which to choose, from tiny shrimps (*crevettes*) to delicious ray (*raie*) and, of course, herrings. But fish is far from being the exclusive bill of fare – you'll find everything from hamburgers to chop suey, couscous to crêpes, and there are restaurants to suit every pocket, from inexpensive snack bars to haute cuisine restaurants where you can dine in style.

La Liègeoise: one of the town's smartest restaurants and one greatly favoured by the upper echelons of the local business community. The interior is elegant with coral pink tablecloths and potted palms and the menu rather more imaginative than most (bring your dictionary) with a leaning towards nouvelle cuisine – or perhaps it is just an illusion created by the enormous Desvres plates the food is served on. Less expensive than you might imagine. *Rue Monsigny,* ☎ *21 31 61 15. Moderate to expensive.*

La Charlotte: started in 1978 by a young Parisian architect, La Charlotte is a very pretty whitewashed house with blue shutters, window boxes and, on the inside, a lot of intimacy (there's room for around twenty diners on the ground floor and ten upstairs). Very good food with lots of interesting fish dishes, although there are generally too many English people to give it full French flavours. Reservations essential. *Rue du Doyen,* ☎ *21 30 13 08. Moderate.*

La Houblonnière: most famous for its 'menu' of a hundred varieties of beer, spanning Ruddles County from Yorkshire, Trappist Monk's brew from Belgium, Sapporo from Japan, San Miguel from Spain and Singha from Thailand – and, of course, La Façon, the local brew. La Houblonnière is also a restaurant serving excellent dishes of the day. *Rue Monsigny,* ☎ *21 30 55 30. Inexpensive to moderate.*

La Crêperie: you can either take advantage of the 'open-window' service for summer takeaways or step over the huge but very friendly hound lounging in the doorway and sit at one of the few tables inside, where you can relish both sweet and savoury crêpes, washed down with a glass of draft cider in true traditional style. The owner/chef is as friendly as his dog. *Rue de la Lampe,* ☎ *21 30 31 38. Inexpensive.*

La Mer: a speciality fish restaurant, and also a wet fish shop – just look at the displays of lobsters, oysters, scallops, shrimps, mussels, sea snails, winkles and crabs before making up your mind. *Rue Faidherbe,* ☎ *21 31 91 25. Moderate.*

Chez Jules: this busy, efficient brasserie restaurant-cum-pizzeria is a long-time favourite with British visitors. The pizzas are cooked on the spot in a wood-fired oven (though they are not available between 2.30 and 7.30 p.m.). The à la carte menu in the restaurant is enormous but there are also very good value fixed-price menus. Chez Jules stays open very late and is one of the best places in town for soaking up and savouring the local night colours. *Pl. Dalton*, ☎ *21 31 54 12*. *Inexpensive to moderate.*

La Plage: this family-run restaurant-hotel tends to get very crowded at lunchtime, both with local residents and the relatively few tourists who have either been recommended it by friends or who accidentally come across it en route to the beach − which is just across the road, hence the name. Tightly packed tables in an unpretentious, no-nonsense setting, and very enjoyable food at reasonable prices. *Blvd Ste Beuve*, ☎ *21 31 45 35*. *Inexpensive to moderate.*

Hamiot: loaded with Gallic atmosphere, this bustling, no-frills café/bar/brasserie is conveniently located at your first 'point of entry' for the town; if your ferry arrives just before lunchtime you really need look no further. You can expect a vigorous blend of customers, from British day-trippers to local fishermen in gumboots, overalls and woolly hats, plus speedy waiters who have a tendency to greet their friends with a well-aimed sugarlump launched from across the bar. Despite the high spirits (there's a quieter upstairs if you prefer) it is a very well run establishment with a robust menu. *Rue Faidherbe*, ☎ *21 31 44 20*. *Inexpensive to moderate.*

An Bascaille Là: lurking in the heart of the old town, in a corner of the main square opposite the Hôtel de Ville, this small restaurant is very popular with British visitors and serves unpretentious dishes, some with a creole influence, at reasonable prices and on outside tables in fine weather. *Pl. Godefroy de Bouillon*, ☎ *21 80 57 30*. *Inexpensive to moderate.*

Haute Ville: well patronised by tourists, this basic French bistro is in the Old Town, easily found, opposite the cathedral in what is reputedly the oldest building in Boulogne. Large helpings and speedy service are its hallmarks. There are several outside tables in the rear courtyard (walk through the archway, past the dovecote), an essential choice for hot weather when the restaurant can feel like a casserole. *Rue de Lille*, ☎ *21 80 54 10*. *Inexpensive to moderate.*

Le Matelote: owner/chef Tony Lestienne's thoroughly modern restaurant earns more praise from the food buffs on both sides of the Channel than any of his competitors in town – and almost the rest of northern France. Michelin-starred, it's the place for a special occasion and for the best of fish dishes à la carte and à la nouvelle cuisine. *Blvd Ste Beuve,* ☎ *21 30 17 97. Expensive.*

Nuts and Bolts

Sealink operate ferry crossings from Folkestone (several are linked to rail timetables between London and Paris, less than $2\frac{1}{2}$ hours away) as well as occasional services from Dover. Townsend Thoresen leave exclusively from Dover. There are also daily Hoverspeed flights from Dover. Ferry around 100 minutes, hovercraft 40 minutes.

Foot passengers arriving on the ferry are deposited on the town's doorstep via an aerial undercover walkway that has been specially designed for handicapped visitors, with gentle slopes and lifts.

Motorists can avoid the central area entirely by taking a direct route from either the hoverport or ferry terminal. This route, which bypasses both the town and its suburbs, is also clearly indicated on the return journey: just look for the distinctive signs as you approach – blue for the ferry, red for the hoverport. A newly opened connection between the port and the N42 has also helped speed up the process of through traffic.

Motorists heading for Paris can choose to follow either the 'no toll' route which is now mostly dual carriageway or pick up the autoroute by following the blue A26/Péage/St Omer signpost which will take you straight through the town and on to Lillers where you can pick up the autoroute. Boulogne is also an important terminal for Motorail services for those wanting to let the train take the strain out of driving to southerly destinations.

The office of the Syndicat d'Initiative is situated at the end of the passenger walkway in the Gare Maritime.

Around and About

In one sense at least the countryside around Boulogne has only recently been given a sense of identity. For the last century it lacked a name to differentiate it from its neighbours but it has now been officially defined as the Pays d'Opale. The region broadly encompasses the contrasting elegance of Le Touquet with the tranquillity of timeless Boulonnais villages dotted with oak and elm forests, the romance of historic Montreuil with the genteel appeal of Wimereux, the cries of the fishermen at Etaples with the fun and games of the massive Bagatelle amusement park. It is not, of course, an original title since the coast, both north and south of Boulogne, from Le Touquet up past Cap Gris Nez has always been known as the Côte d'Opale. Unlike the shingle-bound resorts on the opposite side of the Channel, here you'll find sand dunes and broad swathes of golden beach as well as small seaside villages.

Le Touquet

Created just over 100 years ago by the wealthy English aristocracy who flocked here to inhale lungfuls of healthy air and made it a fashionable resort, Le Touquet-Paris Plage (to give it its proper name) still attracts the chic and stylish, though today they are mostly Parisians, many of whom have invested in holiday homes. The town boasts some of the smartest and most expensive shops in the area: the main street, rue St Jean, has a positively Parisian air, its boutiques selling everything from haute couture fashions to a luxurious selection of leather goods and children's clothes – there is even a shop for the well-dressed doll! Most of the stores stay open on Sundays, making them an added attraction for the British, mini-break visitor.

No aristocratic resort would be complete without a gambling house for the idle rich. Le Touquet has two, the elegant Casino de la Forêt and the Casino des Quatre Saisons, both offering traditional roulette and blackjack. Popular throughout the year with TV and film starlets is the Thalassotherapy Centre at the foot of the promenade, neatly slotted between the Novotel and Ibis hotels. But for sporting enthusiasts of a more energetic variety, there are indoor and outdoor tennis courts, a sailing club, one of the best golf courses along this stretch of coastline and the new Aqualud water-sports complex on the seafront promenade which has a spectacular waterchute housed in a mountain volcano. And don't forget the wide, flat and pristine beach, the setting for land-yachting as well as land-lying, and the landscaped promenade.

Le Manoir Hôtel: a three-star, Tudor-style hotel situated just off one of the beautiful tree-lined roads leading into Le Touquet, Le Manoir has large bedrooms, large bathrooms and prices to match. The food is cooked by the ex-chef of the Royal Crescent Hotel in Bath. Outside are a swimming pool, tennis courts and Le Touquet's three excellent golf courses. *Av. du Golf,* ☎ *21 05 20 22. Moderate to expensive.*

Westminster Hôtel: before you eat at Flavio's, check in at this imposing, old-established four-star hotel, a stone's throw away. It's well worth staying here just for the massively dignified and old-fashioned bathrooms – though the plumbing can be a bit vociferous – and it makes a perfect base for a special-treat weekend. Its massive proportions include 145 rooms, a sauna and a solarium. *Av. du Verger,* ☎ *21 05 19 66. Expensive.*

Flavio: highly rated by Michelin and with a reputation that extends up and down the coast, this paradise of sparkling crystal, pink linen and bowls of silk flowers has for many people become synonymous with Le Touquet. It is owned by Flavio Cucco, an ex-pat Englishman who left his home shores thirty-six years ago to practise gastronomy and Gallic charm, and now enthusiastically guides his British guests round the intricacies of his superb menus. *Av. du Verger* ☎ *21 05 10 22. Moderate to expensive.*

Desvres

When the people of Desvres sing the praises of their 'crockeries' they are not referring to the more ageing or doddery of the town's four thousand inhabitants. Situated just 17 kilometres south-east of Boulogne, Desvres is globally famous for its ceramics. Six potteries produce fine, hand-crafted and painted pottery, ranging from beautifully styled plates and other tableware to wall tiles and display pieces of monumental proportions, as well as items such as chess sets, ornamental violins, birdcages, beer taps, chandeliers and other objects that you never dreamt could be made from such raw ingredients. Most of the potteries are open to visitors and represented by shops in the town's pretty main square (among them Céramiques Desvroises and Céramiques Geo Martel, both open on Sundays). The Desvres brand of ceramics, known as *faience*, has been produced here since Roman times. The distinctive shapes and styles – highly ornate and brilliantly coloured, though varying in detailed style according to the individual pottery – range in price from about 30 francs for a pretty eggcup to about 10,000 francs for a grandly elaborate Ali Baba-type vase.

Chez Mémère Harle: although there are a few good-value eateries, such as Café Jules on the main square in town, you can combine a visit to Desvres with more gastronomic dining at the modest little Chez Mémère Harle café/restaurant between Boulogne and Desvres, in Wirwignes. Try Mme Louchez's traditional home-baked local speciality – custard tart (each November the town holds a custard tart festival). *Wirwignes,* ☎ *21 91 71 82. Inexpensive to moderate.*

Hostellerie du Château des Tourelles: again out of town, in the hills, this renovated nineteenth-century little château hotel run by a young couple, Michelle and Serge Feutry, is extremely comfortable. There are sixteen attractive bedrooms and a smart, good-value restaurant, where you can find cheeses on the menu supplied by Philippe Olivier. *Le Wast,* ☎ *21 33 34 78. Moderate.*

Montreuil

Montreuil-sur-Mer, despite its name, is *sur mer* no longer. The sea invaded the valley of the river Canche several epochs ago, enabling Montreuil to flourish as a harbour until the sixteenth century, becoming a place of some importance with a population of more than 40,000. Today the number of inhabitants has dwindled to just 3000 and the only ships you'll see on the river are sporty kayaks. The sea has receded a dozen or so kilometres to the west and the lands that once lay under the ocean are now thick with poplars which help to drain the still marshy lands as well as give the valley its beautiful appearance.

Montreuil is steeped in history. Enjoying a dramatic hilltop position, it was first fortified with protective ramparts by the ancient Gauls and then strengthened by the Romans, but it is best known for its red-brick, cliff-like walls, first laid out in the tenth century and extended in the sixteenth. Up here you have a ready-made stroll along the crest, a three-kilometre route offering stunning views over the Canche valley and the surrounding rolling countryside.

History buffs will particularly relish a visit to the citadel – look out for the commemorative list of local heroes who gave their lives in battle, not in the Second or even the First World War, but in the battle of Agincourt against Henry V, more than five centuries ago. There is also the thirteenth-century Benedictine Abbey of St Saulve with a distinctive leaning column in the aisle, a wound inflicted during an earthquake in 1537.

Château de Montreuil: the smartest hotel and restaurant for miles around, this beautiful blue-shuttered mansion stands in tranquil gardens below the city ramparts. Belonging to the highly upmarket Relais et Châteaux group, it is now owned by Christian Germain who has imported his fine skills learned when he was head chef at the Waterside Inn at Bray, one of Britain's finest restaurants. The proof of the pudding, so to speak, lies in Monsieur Germain's gourmet menu which offers no choices 'but lots of surprises'. There are fourteen charming double rooms, some up in the garrets, most on the first floor. *Chaussée des Capucins,* ☎ *21 81 53 04. Expensive.*

Hôtel de France: built in 1600 as a coaching inn to serve passengers (and horses) on the Paris–Boulogne run, the Hôtel de France has changed little on the outside. In the cobbled courtyard there is a huge oil painting depicting the arrival of the Yorkshire vicar Laurence Sterne, who stayed at the hotel in 1765 on his Sentimental Journey to the Court of France and no doubt used some of the still-remaining antique furniture to store his clothes and rest his bones. The adjacent restaurant, the Relais du Roy, is under separate ownership but recommended for its inexpensive menus and giant log fire in winter. *Rue Pierre Ledent,* ☎ *21 06 05 36. Inexpensive to moderate.*

Wimereux

Only a five-minute bus ride up the coast from Boulogne, this genteel seaside town has always been popular with British families, but their discriminating presence does not detract from the wholesome French flavour of the town. A warm, shallow pool, some 55 metres long, which gathers on the wide, flat expanse of sandy beach at low tide, is excellent for children, and their parents can sit on the prom, sipping a kir at the tables of the presiding Hotel Atlantic, watching the ferries drift in and out of the port and the hovercraft roar past (sometimes it seems a little too close to the shore for comfort).

Even out of season there is plenty to do in Wimereux – fishing (sea and river), tennis, sailing, windsurfing and excellent golf – with all the amenities conveniently placed within walking distance.

Hotel Atlantic: a most solid seaside establishment dominating the seafront, with café tables and chairs spilling across the promenade. It has been well patronised by the British for generations, not so much for its rooms, which have nothing special except the view, but for its Michelin-rosette restaurant specialising in such fish dishes as *bar braisé au champagne. Digue de Mer,* ☎ *21 32 41 01. Moderate to expensive.*

Hôtel du Centre: Jean-Marc Boulanger and family run this very French, very cosy and very friendly hotel in the main shopping street of Wimereux. The emphasis throughout is on peace and simplicity. There are two floors of bedrooms, some in a new wing, and they are small but fitted with everything you could need. The chef, Jean-Marc's father (Boulanger le Grand in size and seniority) produces *raie au beurre noir* served with steamed potatoes and mini moules that are the sweetest in the world. In summer you can catch the last rays of the sun in the small back garden or in winter sink into a chair in the lounge with a kir in front of a log fire and the television. *Rue Carnot,* ☎ *21 32 41 08. Inexpensive to moderate.*

La Rencontre: although just a ten-minute cross-country drive from Wimereux, you could easily scoot right past this little *auberge* tucked away in the tiniest hamlet of Hesdres. To avoid disappointment take a map to get you to the best of straightforward rural cuisine, including crêpes and 'ancient waffles' as well as regular meals at modest prices. The original walls of the farmhouse have been left standing so that you can eat in your own dining room. *Hesdres, Wierre-Effroy,* ☎ *21 33 20 72. Inexpensive.*

Marquenterre

If you've never lifted a pair of binoculars to your eyes nor opened the pages of a spotter's guide to the feathered world, the bird sanctuary at Marquenterre is a wonderful place to start. One of the most famous in France, it lies less than an hour's drive south of Boulogne on the RN1 (roughly halfway between Montreuil and Abbeville) and consists of 5000 acres of sand dunes, small lakes, pine forests, marshlands, salt-meadows and scrubland bordering on the bay of the river Somme. On a par with Slimbridge near Bristol, this wetland habitat provides a protected home to about 320 species of birds throughout the year, a staggering quota when you consider that only about 450 have ever been recorded in Europe as a whole. Open daily from the end of March till the beginning of November. Binoculars, by the way, may be hired on the spot.

Hardelot Plage

This resort appropriately describes itself as 'a garden by the sea'. It is a spruce place, well-sited amongst pine forests, lakes and dunes, with an excellent beach, fancy villas and a renowned golf course. Had it been less residential it would have stood a good chance of becoming another Le Touquet. The next-door village, Condette, is where Charles Dickens used to stay with his mistress, the actress Elen Ternan, and where he penned *Bleak House* and *Hard Times*.

Etaples

Talk to any veteran of the First World War and he will be sure to remember Etaples as an important British Army base and military hospital complex. Just outside the town, on your right as you approach from Boulogne, you pass the largest cemetery in northern France where over 10,000 British and Commonwealth troops lie buried. The Tommies might recall the place even better if you refer to it as 'Eat Apples', their nickname for the small town overlooking the river Canche, 5 kilometres across from Le Touquet. Under today's more pleasure-loaded circumstances the British might prefer the more aptly devised nickname of 'Eat Fish' since topping the list of most visitors' priorities is a splendid lunch at one of Etaples' seafood restaurants.

Aux Pêcheurs d'Etaples: owned and run by a fishermen's co-operative and located right on the quayside within yards of the quay where the daily catch is landed, Aux Pêcheurs is the place to feast on sole, turbot, herring, skate, plaice, red mullet and all kinds of shellfish; it offers, as the menu promises, 'an opportunity of tasting the products of the sea and participating in the activities of the promotion of fish'. If you are unsure of your French, take a stroll first around the superb fish shop on the ground floor before sitting down to this briny feast.

Berck

It is hard for British people to react with anything other than a fit of the giggles at the mere mention of the name Berck. But even though this seaside resort is less fashionable than neighbouring Le Touquet, it deserves to be taken just as seriously. For example, its beach is a pure delight, a 12-kilometre swathe of pure sand without a trace of mud or a pebble to spoil its good looks. It gets a regular, twice-daily wash from the sea, too, so you won't find a shred of litter – indeed, it is reckoned to be one of the cleanest and most beautiful beaches in Europe. Visitors have long sung the praises of Berck's invigorating air and ozone, a micro-climate that has drawn large numbers of the frail and convalescing, especially those with bone conditions, and there are centres here especially for them. Other things of interest to see in Berck include scores of small fishermen's cottages, the all-wooden church of St John the Baptist (whose church steeple once housed the Berck lighthouse) and the new Agora water-sport centre.

Bagatelle

A massive 60-acre amusement park, France's answer to Disney-land, with a zoo, boat hire, miniature-train rides, a monorail, go-karts and various cafés, bars and restaurants. Open from March till the end of September, Bagatelle is on the D940 between Etaples and Le Touquet at Merlimont.

The Road to Agincourt

This route takes a full day and leads you along some of the delightful secondary roads south-east of Boulogne. Take the N1 to Samer, less than ten miles away, and then fork off on the D125 for Parenty, a small village with a fine château. Cross the Valley of the Course, a pleasant stream, to pass by several lakes (with good fishing), pretty cottages and tiny inns along the way (some even unknown to the Boulonnaise); then take the D148 to Hucqueliers, and continue on this road to the picturesque and little-visited Valley of the Aa at Verchocq. Once here, you will pick up the sign for Fruges, a small market town at the bottom of a steep hill, which has several cafés in the main square. If you want to stay here try the Logis de France one-star Hôtel Moderne, ☎ 21 04 41 98.

The road to Agincourt is the main D928 which leads south to Ruisseauville, where the D104 takes you to three villages: the château at Tramecourt is still lived in by the family who have owned a castle on this site since the eleventh century (unfortunately the present château is not open to visitors); Maisoncelle marks the spot where Henry V's troops spent the night before the Battle of Agincourt, the eve of the feast day of St Crispin and St Crispian in 1415 (the King himself, contrary to popular belief, did not mingle chummily with his men that night but stayed at nearby Blangy-sur-Ternoise). The three villages border the open land of the scene of one of the bloodiest battles in English history in which Henry V killed or took prisoner 10,000 of the French nobility. The actual battlefield lies to the right, just before the Azincourt-Tramecourt crossroads and the clump of trees on the left, with the cròss, marks the original grave pits.

It will take an hour or so to explore the battlefield, and ride down to Tramecourt. Unless you take a picnic it is better to lunch in Hesdin, an attractive old town sprawling at the foot of forest-covered hills and the location of many *Maigret* episodes. If you happen to be here on a Thursday morning you'll catch one of the best markets in France – it's held in the main square in front of the town hall, flanked by picturesque arcades, and sells everything possible – flowers, food, spices, clothes, basketry, artworks. . . . We recommend you eat here at the Rôtisserie des Flandres, whose specialities include *coquilles St-Jacques*, sole, trout and various regional dishes. There are also rooms to be rented in this two-star Logis de France. Drive back in the afternoon along the Valley of the Canche and after tea at Montreuil return to Boulogne.

Caen

For the arriving ferry passenger, Caen may at first seem a bit of a con. Although billed as France's newest Channel port, the Brittany Ferries from Portsmouth actually dock in Ouistreham, a small town at the mouth of the river Orne, connected to Caen by 15 kilometres of fast, newly built dual-carriageway. The ferries could continue up the 4-kilometre canal that runs parallel with the river Orne and deposit their cargo, along with the rest of Caen's annual maritime traffic of nearly two million tons, right in the heart of town, but a series of locks would have to be negotiated – hardly a practical proposition for a ferry service.

France's twelfth most important port has certainly been given a welcome boost by the new ferry route. Although the majority of passengers will no doubt use Ouistreham just as a gateway to the south, particularly to the Loire Valley, a few days spent in Caen, capital of Lower Normandy and right in the heart of Calvados countryside, are well worth considering. Today's large, lively, modern, cultural centre, with a population of 120,000, started life as a tiny settlement at the confluence of the rivers Odon and Orne, destined to be nurtured, protected and fortified by William the Bastard, latterly known as the Conqueror, in the eleventh century. In fact, rumour has it that because he loved Normandy he created Caen in order to stay there and his name has remained synonymous with the town's ever since. In 1987, 900 years after his death, the town will be ablaze with festivities and celebrations.

Although fortified by the early Normans and full of beautiful abbeys and churches, nearly three-quarters of the town was laid waste in two months of heavy bombing by the British and Canadians when attempting to reclaim the sea-port in 1944, and later by the retreating Germans. But although much of the town's historic beauty was lost, a lot of time, money and energy was spent on Caen's renaissance so that today remains of historical buildings stand at ease alongside hi-tech edifices, mostly built of the same soft, mellow, honey-coloured, local limestone which was earlier shipped to England by William the Conqueror and used for Canterbury Cathedral and the Tower of London. Caen has been designed with a sense of spatial generosity; it is landscaped with parks, attractive pedestrianised streets, broad avenues lined with some 31,000 newly planted trees, and even a racecourse bang in the centre in an area called La Prairie which is an arm of surrounding countryside that penetrates deep into the heart of town. Not surprisingly, Caen is known as the *ville verte* and is classified as the second 'ecological' town of France.

The town's youthful, bubbling atmosphere – 45 per cent of the population are less than twenty-five years old – owes much to its university, founded by Henry VI in 1432 (he went on to build King's College, Cambridge, a decade later). Rebuilt as a modern architectural masterpiece, covering some 80 acres north of town behind the castle, it attracts over 12,000 students. Since youth implies active leisure, Caen also has more than 100 sports clubs and a high profile of bars and nightclubs.

Do Not Miss

When you look at a map of Caen, spread across the page in gulping proportions, it looks an alarming prospect for the visitor. But despair not. The suburbs sprawl for miles and everything worth seeing is contained within a square mile immediately south of the castle.

The Pope strongly disapproved of the strong blood link between William the Conqueror and his wife, his cousin Matilda of Flanders, and excommunicated the couple shortly after their marriage. The only way William could win back Papal approval was by promising to found an abbey exclusively for men and Matilda promising to do the same for women. The **Abbaye aux Hommes** (St Etienne) and **Abbaye aux Dames** (La Trinité) are the magnificent results of their promises, earning Caen the title of 'Norman Athens'.

Both were built in Normandy's predominating eleventh-century Romanesque style and finished off in Gothic a century later. The abbey church of St Etienne is a superb example of High Romanesque, a style that William's Prior-cum-Secretary Lanfranc, the builder of Aux Hommes, modified when he carried it over the Channel and built Canterbury Cathedral. Throughout the Battle of Caen the Allies deliberately avoided bombing the two abbey churches, aware from the Resistance that hundreds of local residents were using them for refuge: in fact 1500 were living in the Abbaye aux Hommes, and the Abbaye aux Dames was being used as a hospital and hospice.

Although William died in Rouen, he was buried within the Abbey's sanctuary 900 years ago, beneath an imposing tomb on which he is described as Duke of Normandy and King of England – in that order (his remains were stolen from the tomb by the Huguenots in the sixteenth century and later tossed into the river by the Revolutionaries, leaving only a thigh bone to be later discovered). You can still see the greater part of the original building, including the nave, the transept and the lantern tower, though part of the original Abbey – the adjacent conventual building housing the parlour, cloister, refectory, chapter house, main staircase and guard room – is now the city hall and is only open for guided tours. Set back from the square, its flag-lined driveway, huge manicured gardens and picturesque flower beds give the building the airs of a palace rather than a local government HQ.

Queen Matilda's Abbaye aux Dames, with its sixteen massive-pillared crypt, is a more compact building, rebuilt in the classical style in the seventeenth century. You can visit Matilda's tomb in the choir part of the church. It stands on the other side of town, about a kilometre from Aux Hommes, and, after years of faithful service as an old people's home, the Abbey is now also a local government building, newly restored, and, since January 1986, open to visitors for the first time. Matilda's tomb lies in the choir of the church of La Trinité whose elegant spires were sadly destroyed in the war.

In contrast to the austerity of the abbeys, the Renaissance left its architectural mark principally on the highly ornamented **St Pierre**, the parish church of the city merchants. Its original 80-metre-high belfry caught a direct hit from a shell fired by HMS *Rodney* but was later reconstructed.

The **Church of St-Jean**, just off the place de la Résistance, is Caen's Tower of Pisa lookalike – it was never completed because of the surrounding unstable marshes, and today the whole church leans rather unnervingly, as do the pillars inside.

High up above the town, situated halfway between the two abbeys, William's eleventh-century **castle** is easily spotted as you enter Caen from Ouistreham. Its bold appearance, like some craggy grey mountain rising from a sea of neatly trimmed grass and flower beds, still proudly flying the Norman flag (two leopards against a red background), is paradoxically enhanced by the wartime disappearance of the buildings that once surrounded it. Cross the drawbridge, pass under the ramparts (the longest in France at 1.3 kilometres) and once inside you'll find a surprise of trees, gardens, a children's play area, and two museums. The **Musée des Beaux Arts** has impressive galleries of Italian, Flemish and French painters, including Veronese, Tintoretto, Rubens, Poussin, Monet and Bonnard. There are enamels from Limoges, eighteenth-century miniatures, tapestries and an exceptional collection of 50,000 engravings including works by Dürer and Rembrandt. The **Musée de Normandie** is housed in the old Governor's House and describes Normandy through the ages with scale models of farms, field layouts, machinery, costumes, crafts and a detailed study of how the rural folk worked, from the making of buttons to boxes for Camembert. Also within the walls are the **Hall of Exchequer, St George's Chapel** and a **Jardin des Simples** filled with examples of medical and aromatic plants which were cultivated in the Middle Ages.

Dotted around town you'll stumble across several **Hôtels Particuliers**. One, the sixteenth-century Hôtel d'Escoville, houses the Tourist Information Centre; another good example is the Hôtel de Taon. They are the surviving examples of beautiful Renaissance private mansions that were once owned by the nobility and that are a striking reminder of how beautiful a town Caen must have been before the war.

Halfway down rue St-Pierre, in one of the town's ancient half-timbered buildings, is the **Musée de la Poste et des Techniques de Communication** which tells the story of Lower Normandy's communication system, as well as explaining future innovations.

The Museum of the Battle of Normandy has yet to be built but the first stones, one from each country involved in the famous battle, were laid in September 1986. As well as being a Second World War research centre the museum will deal with all aspects of the battle, discuss strategies and display the equipment and documents used as well as portraits of those who took part. It is scheduled to open in June 1988.

Shopping Spree

Caen calls for sensible shoes as well as laden wallets, since the shops are in glorious abundance and seem to run from street to street without respite. Second to Paris it is the best city in northern France for spending money. Head first for the town's biggest square, place de la République, and you'll find yourself at the hub of all the main shopping streets, particularly rue St-Pierre (the largest) and rue St Jean (both signposted from when you first enter town), the pedestrianised rue Froide lined mostly with clothes shops housed in sixteenth-century buildings, and rue de Bernières. And save time for the area called Le Vaugueux, the Covent Garden of Caen, just below the castle. With the atmosphere of an artisan *quartier*, rue du Vaugueux is cobbled and pedestrianised, lined with old half-timbered buildings. It has a few antique shops, *boulangeries* and *pâtisseries*, a lot of bars, pavement cafés and restaurants, all set against a stage-set backdrop of a medieval epoch.

Nicolas: an excellent stock of wines, but wherever you park you'll have a long walk carrying your crates. *Rue Bellivet*.

Printemps: a large specimen of the breed just where you'd expect to find it, in one of Caen's main shopping streets and opposite the church of St Sauveur. *Rue St-Pierre*. The town's other department stores – **Nouvelles Galeries, Bon Marché, Monoprix**, and **C & A** – are grouped around the centrally located *Blvd Maréchal-Leclerc*.

La Forêt Magique: an impressive array of clothes, shoes and cuddly toys for children up to 12 years. Particularly cute are the tiny bikinis and the matching sweatshirts and dungaree sets. *Blvd Maréchal-Leclerc*.

Lagnel-Tastemain: if you want to go home with a sense of Caen's history, have a browse around this shop's old engravings both of the town and the rest of Normandy, including posters of the *Normandie*'s inaugural voyage from Le Havre to New York in 1935. *Blvd Maréchal-Leclerc*.

Hédiard: under the canopy of the Cours des Halles, this *épicerie* displays a huge array of fruit, vegetables, garlic, artichokes, cheeses, own-label mustards, honey and jam, almond biscuits, teas and wines. Delicious slabs of their home-made sweets lie ready-cut into tiny squares. *Corner of rue Exmoisne and Blvd Maréchal-Leclerc*.

Marc Eustache: this master cheesemaker sells farm Appellation Originie Livarot, Pont-l'Evêque and goats' cheeses displayed on small pine tables. *Rue des Chanoines*.

Brion: the two girls who run this perfumery are as immaculate, smart and trendy as the hi-tech décor, and the shelves are stocked with every scent under the sun (well, almost). There are four branches in Caen, this one in *rue St-Pierre*.

Hottot Chocolatier: to satisfy the most insatiable of chocolate cravings, this shop produces its own speciality chocolates – Les Drakkars – made from a deliciously light, soft *mousse praline meringue*. *Rue St-Pierre*.

Bon Appetit: this shop calls itself an *artisan charcuterie* and certainly the display of sausage, house tripe, salads, duck and pheasant pâtés looks like a work of art. Try their individual brioches stuffed with scallops and other *fruits de mer*. *Rue St-Pierre*.

Au Rayon de Soleil: there are clothes shops galore in Caen but children seem to do exceptionally well. If you know the Petit Bateau range, you'll recognise the simple, dainty-looking, pastel-coloured clothes on sale here. *Rue St-Pierre*.

Jane d'Herval: she recently transported her collection and staff a few doors down the road to a bigger and better shop but still sells what must be the most expensive and elegant ladies' silk clothes in town. *Rue St-Pierre.*

Aux Ducs de Gascogne: an enticing food store specialising in *confits, foie gras* and other specialities from south-west France, all packed in elegant black tins with white and gold labels – excellent for presents. *Rue de Strasbourg.*

Salisbury's: an anglified shop selling Burberrys but also smart tailored men's and women's suits, expensive woollens, scarves and bags. *Rue de Strasbourg.*

L'Herbier: everything in this shop is made from herbs and is for spoiling yourself in the bathroom – hence the sweet-smelling perfume of soaps as you walk in. Beyond the stands of luxury, healthy toiletries there are also jars of herbal teas. *Rue Froide.*

Maison de la Presse: Caen's source of English newspapers. *Rue St Jean.*

Geneviève Lethu: Marie et Bernard Lanfray say their shop sells '*des objets pour être bien chez soi*', which sums it up pretty well. Under one roof you'll find every glass, plate, cup, breadboard and salt-cellar the modern homemaker could ever need. *Rue St Jean.*

Pom d'Api: if there are such things as avant-garde boots, you'll find them here – French, elegant, three-quarter-length cowboy styles in bright colours. Also a strong line in 'Little Mary' very pretty, coloured leather shoes for tiny feet. *Rue St Jean.*

Doumick: a small, craftsmen-run infants' shop with beautiful hand-made wooden toys including puppets and skittles. *Rue Montoir-Poissonerie.*

Heiz Legrix: picnickers are spoilt for choice here – there are twenty-one different types of bread on sale (hence the queues out on the street). *Blvd des Alliés.*

C.C.V.: a pair of shops affiliated to the university, one for men, one for women. They are cheerful, hectic and colourful emporiums of smart but casual clothes (a good line in men's Sabre sweaters), jewellery, shoes and accessories. *Blvd des Alliés.*

Sweaterie: this branch stocks fashionable, designer-label sweat-shirts, satin sweatshirts, sweatshirts with collars and plainer sweatshirts at lower prices – just sift through the piles on the shelves or rummage through the bargain barrel. *Rue du Moulin.*

Brune: the stock in M. Brune's shop, which stands just a few yards from the Palais de Justice, is a mish-mash of interesting collectables including antiques, jewellery, Bayeux lace, carved ivory, second-hand books and old hats. *Rue Ecuyère.*

Martine Lambert: all you can buy here are sorbets and ice-creams – but in such flamboyant flavours as almond and honey, apricot with Armagnac, cassis and passion fruit and nut nougatine. *Rue de Bernières.*

Hypermarkets: Champion is Ouistreham's brand-new hyper-market, built as a magnet for the newly arrived (or about to depart) ferry passengers just on the road to Caen. But there are others including **Carrefour**, the biggest, at Hérouville, an unattractive but functional modern 'estate'-looking town on your right as you drive to Caen. For foot passengers, the Bus Verts (green buses), *ligne 1*, run regularly from the ferry terminal to Caen (the journey takes twenty-five minutes) and stops at Hérouville near Carrefour (from Hérouville you can hop onto the next green bus or any of the regular yellow, orange and white town buses which run roughly every fifteen minutes to the centre of town). There are also two **Le Continents**, one at Mondeville in the direction of Lisieux and the other at Côte de Nacre, at the entrance to Caen when you arrive on the road from Luc sur Mer.

Caen's main **market** is a colourful, open-air event held every Friday; stalls overflow with fresh fruit and vegetables, flowers and cheeses, strung out along both sides of Fosses St Julien all the way to place St Sauveur.

The smaller **St Pierre market** is held every Sunday in place Courtonne near the Bassin St Pierre; it sells mainly antiques, but there are also stalls piled with fruit and vegetables and a few with clothes.

During the first week in July Caen is lost amid its annual *braderie*: two days of feverish sales in the shops, whose windows tend to be hidden by hundreds of stalls, street traders and milling crowds.

A Place to Stay

You shouldn't have any problem finding a room in Caen, not only because it has more than its fair quota of hotels, but also because a large proportion of visitors stay in resorts along the coast and in nearby touristy Bayeux.

Ma Normandie: the nine rooms in this eighteenth-century house have a tried-and-tested track record with the English who, according to the owner, come back year after year (star guest was a girl student who returned years later as a married woman). *Rue Ecuyère,* ☎ *31 86 13 53. Inexpensive.*

Moderne: a three-star hotel that has been rebuilt in the acceptable face of Caen's post-war reconstruction and has been in the same family for fifty-four years. The welcome by Mme Jacqueline Mabille and her team is friendly enough but once beyond the reception area the atmosphere becomes rather soulless and international. The fifty-seven rooms have all the cons required by the businessman. The cosmopolitan flavour is enhanced by the Four Seasons restaurant which is decorated Italian style, with countryside murals and flowers on the tables. Chef Philippe Errard's house specialities are printed in bold type on the menu. *Blvd Maréchal-Leclerc,* ☎ *31 86 04 23. Expensive.*

Mercure: this member of the French mega-chain has 101 fully equipped rooms and is centrally located by the marina St-Pierre, close to all the points of interest as well as, presumably, business meetings. *Rue de Courtonne,* ☎ *31 93 07 62. Expensive.*

De La Paix: a one-star, right-where-you-want-to-be hotel with rooms hidden behind window-boxes of geraniums. In a side street but with probably less *calme* than promised. *Rue Neuve St-Jean,* ☎ *31 86 18 99. Inexpensive to moderate.*

Saint Laurent: in a quiet road just off place St-Sauveur, and well deserving of its one star. If you can't get any answer from the main doorway just carry on twenty yards to the corner bar/brasserie, which belongs to the same family and gives the rather humdrum sleeping section a bit of oomph. *Rue St Laurent*, ☎ *31 86 07 39. Inexpensive to moderate.*

Royal: the dilemma here is whether to opt for the quieter but smaller rooms at the back of the house or the larger ones at the front overlooking rue Strasbourg and the place de la République. There are forty-five rooms in this prestigious location, but no restaurant. *Pl. de la République*, ☎ *31 86 55 33. Moderate.*

Le Dauphin: M. et Mme Robert Chabredier, by far the nicest hotel keepers we met in town, run this France Accueil three-star hotel in a building that dates back to William the Conqueror, when it was a priory. It opened as a hotel in 1966 and within a short time gained high accolades for its restaurant which is featured in a book on Normandy gastronomy. Lobster in cider and the local tripe dish are two of the specialities to be relished in front of the open fire in the elegant dining room. There are twenty-one smart rooms as well as a bar built out of the remains of a cider press. *Rue Gémare*, ☎ *31 86 22 26. Moderate.*

And Somewhere to Eat

Caen competes with Rouen as the gastronomic capital of Normandy, producing one of France's most famous dishes, *tripes à la mode de Caen*. The dish, made from tripe and calves' feet – to which vegetables, garlic, herbs and cider are added – was perfected in the fourteenth century by a chef called Benoit and the recipe has changed little since. Other Normandy menu specialities to look out for include *poulet vallée d'Auge, sole Normandie*, the Livarot, Camembert and Pont l'Evêque cheeses and *pâté de lapin* (farms in the region are overrun with rabbits).

Restaurant Louis XIV and **Brasserie Hôtel de Ville:** an elegant first-floor restaurant, the Louis XIV bit; all the tables are set with tall white candles ready to illuminate veal kidneys in an ancient-recipe mustard sauce and other dishes that make the Restaurant

Louis XIV a gastronomic high-spot in town; the more informal brasserie downstairs has an unadventurous but good-value menu including huge salads (ideal for lunch) and six types of kir (not so ideal for lunch). The proprietors are in the process of transforming the rooms into a hotel scheduled to open in January 1987. *Pl. St-Sauveur,* ☎ *31 86 11 93. Inexpensive to moderate brasserie, moderate to expensive restaurant.*

Bar du Palais: another pair of restaurants; the top floor is a very straightforward, no-nonsense restaurant, and the downstairs is a brasserie-cum-bar under separate ownership where you can get pizza, quiche and sandwiches. *Pl. Fontette (no telephone). Inexpensive brasserie, inexpensive to moderate restaurant.*

La Bourride: *'La cuisine, comme la femme, a besoin d'amour et d'attention'*, says owner Michel Bruneau, but don't let his sexist attitude to cooking put you off. He and his wife Françoise use a lot of local ingredients including pigeon, fish, goose and apples. *Bourride à ma façon* is the house speciality – one of their huge, daintily designed octagonal plates piled high with poached *fruits de mer* and fresh vegetables. Situated in a prime spot, La Bourride is more expensive than most. Try to get a table on the minstrel-gallery-type upper floor with its coloured velvet chairs, copper pans and photos of pierrots hanging from the stone walls, pink tablecloths and exposed wooden beams; tiny windows open onto a geranium-filled roof garden in summer, and in winter a cosy fire blazes. *Rue du Vaugueux,* ☎ *31 93 50 76. Expensive.*

La Mandarine: a richly decorated, slightly over-the-top establishment in one of the oldest, cobble-paved, streets in town, already existing at the time of William the Conqueror. Chirpy Mme Cherel has, within a short time of ownership, created a good reputation for her Nantais-style cooking of mostly fish dishes. *Rue Froide,* ☎ *31 85 39 97. Moderate.*

Couscous Royal: in a prime position at the top of Le Vaugueux, this is Caen's most upmarket ethnic restaurant, serving part-Spanish, part-North African cuisine (Arabic couscous and Spanish paella are the two speciality dishes, the former served with Merguez sausages, the latter with shrimps, prawns, mussels, chicken, sausage and squid). Wash both down with a glass of Algerian, Moroccan or

Tunisian wine. The enthusiastic Tunisian owner and his son both speak good English and the décor is evocatively Islamic with pointed arches, Algerian paintings and high-backed chairs in the restaurant, and mosaic tiles polished to perfection in the loos. *Rue du Vaugueux*, ☎ *31 93 54 12.* Their other restaurant, **Au Tassili**, is on the other side of town in *rue Jules Oyer,* ☎ *31 82 35 12. Moderate.*

Les Echevins: a serious dining experience, as they say, in the capable hands of Paris-trained Patrick Regnier. Varied repertoire, though the actual choices are limited, with an emphasis on highly personal sauces. *Rue Ecuyère,* ☎ *31 86 37 44. Moderate to expensive.*

Nuts and Bolts

Brittany Ferries operate once- and twice-daily crossings (depending on the month) from Portsmouth to Ouistreham. Journey time is approximately 5¾ hours. Brittany Ferries, ☎ Portsmouth 0705 827701 or Caen 31 96 80 80.

Although Caen is a new ferry port there is no excuse for the disastrous lack of signposts for motorists as they leave Ouistreham, · which causes half the newly arrived vehicles to get into the wrong lane and have to swing left across more purposefully moving commercial traffic as they leave the terminal area.

Having disembarked in Ouistreham, foot passengers can catch a Bus Vert, whose timetables coincide with the arrival of the ferries, to Caen's bus station next to the railway station, a good fifteen-minute walk from the town centre. Return buses are also scheduled so that they arrive in Ouistreham in time for the departing ferry.

Parking is a nightmare unless you manage to find a vacant meter in the elegant place St-Sauveur, so leave the car on the perimeter and walk in.

The Office de Tourisme is in place St-Pierre, and is open on Sundays during the summer (☎ 31 86 27 65).

Around and About

Spread all about Caen's doorstep, yet barely touched by British visitors, is the very pretty region of Calvados. Named after an outcrop of rocks that lies off the coast (whose name, in turn, is an almost unrecognisable derivation of '*San Salvador*', one of Spanish King Philip II's ships that survived the Armada only to come to grief on the rocks), Calvados today is synonymous with apple brandy. But the area's hideaways, sadly often bypassed by motorists who take the motorway from Caen direct to Paris, deserve more than a passing tipple or two.

The region of Calvados lies between the rivers Vire and Seine and includes the Pays d'Auge south of Deauville and the Suisse Normande area around the river Orne. It is fringed to the north by the broad, pan-flat, sandy expanses of the Côte de Nacre, the Mother of Pearl coast, often swept by bracing winds, and famous for its oysters (though rarely those with a heart of pearl). To most British people it is more familiar as the chosen theatre for the Second World War landings, but for years the French have descended in family-fun force onto eight charming family-holiday resorts, which offer safe bathing and plenty of natural water-sport facilities. Just south of Caen the river Orne wends its way through the scenic Suisse Normande; while not *quite* as mountainous as its namesake, this pretty, verdant countryside is broken by steep, tree-topped cliffs shaped by the river, the perfect hideaway for walkers, canoeists and fishermen.

Further north you can drive for miles through Calvados along winding empty roads which cut through an agricultural plateau rich in sugar-beet and cereals and dotted with fifteenth- and sixteenth-century half-timbered manor houses, dozy Norman villages and distinctive farmhouses with tall, wedge-shaped, tiled roofs, and high-walled courtyards and turrets; these farms, many of them dairy, are the source of the region's acclaimed products that find their way to the best of Normandy – and Parisian – restaurant tables: *crème fraîche* (sour cream – the key ingredient of *sauce Normande*), Pont l'Evêque, Livarot and squidgy Camembert cheeses, sparkling *cidre bouché*, delicious *tarte aux pommes* and, of course, Calvados apple brandy.

One way to 'do' Calvados is to choose one of the touring themes recommended by the tourist office. Cheese villages, cider farms, D-Day landing beaches and places with William the Conqueror associations are the most interesting options. If you have time on your hands and life in your legs you may prefer to explore Calvados from the abundance of marked footpaths – details of where to find a good hike or two are available from the tourist office in Caen.

Ouistreham Riva-Bella

Ouistreham was a name that rarely rolled off the British tongue until motorists began rolling off the Brittany Ferries when they inaugurated their route from Portsmouth to Caen in 1986. This lively, once almost exclusively French, family seaside town that now bears witness to a steady stream of GB stickers is an important yachting cente at the seaward end of the Caen canal that merges at its northern edge into coastal Riva-Bella.

It is hard to predict just what the centre of Ouistreham will look like when the car ferry works are completed – in July 1986, a month after the ferry route had opened, there were JCBs wallowing in a chaotic choreography all over the place, and the signposting was dreadful. But those who chose to drive to the beach down quiet, tree-lined avenues, or got accidentally misdirected from their planned routes elsewhere, would have found several miles of pale yellow sand, safe bathing, rows of beach huts and happy manoeuvres by bucket, spade and Lilo-armed platoons. Health freaks should head here at low tide when the air is filled with health-giving fumes from the seaweed revealed as the tide recedes two miles.

The hotels, dispersed arbitrarily amongst a grid of modest villas and bungalows in the streets that lie behind the prom, are uninspiring, but, as bases for beach holidays, they seem to be doing a good job.

Hôtel de l'Univers: the grand hotel of the town that, from our experience, did not live up to its reputation or, for our money, its level of prices. The hotel's most endearing features are its convenience (it is bang opposite the fishing port and new ferry terminal), and its popular La Broche d'Argent restaurant which puts on too many airs and graces but does come up with a good à la carte, especially its fish (if in doubt go for the *fruits de mer* hors d'oeuvre, a dish piled high with winkles, cockles, mussels, oysters and crab). The fifty hotel rooms are a definite notch above basic Gallic comfort and, when the dust settles and the noise subsides, those at the front will be very snoozeworthy. *Place du Général de Gaulle,* ☎ *31 97 12 16. Moderate.*

Le Chalet: Proprietor Jacques Chevron is French but his wife, April, comes from Bristol, which explains the pub-type bar and the draught Bass. The hotel has no restaurant (which, with the British stamp everywhere else, might be a blessing) but is conveniently next door to the little Les Tisons restaurant and a few minutes from several others along the seafront. *Av. de la Mer,* ☎ *31 97 12 06. Inexpensive to moderate.*

Bayeux

After the modernity of Caen, Bayeux feels trapped in a time warp. Less than eight miles from the landing beaches, it was the first major town to be liberated by the Allies and luckily escaped serious war damage, leaving many of its Caen limestone houses (some dating from the fourteenth century) beautifully intact along quaint, cobbled shopping streets. This small, ancient and extremely pretty town is the capital of the Bessin, a meadowy, pastoral subsection of Calvados, and is famous for its pottery, lace-making, and its graceful, medieval cathedral, more decorative than Caen's austere abbeys and the best example of Calvados' exuberant, ornate Gothic-Normand architecture. Oh yes, and a tapestry.

In 1066, Guillaume le Bâtard, as he was affectionately known (being the illegitimate son of Robert the Devil) and his fleet of some 800 vessels, the greatest invasion force ever to have crossed the Channel, mounted his successful conquest of Britain. The invasion, and the events leading up to it, are chronicled in what the French call 'La Tapisserie de la Reine Matilde' though it is neither, technically quibbling, a tapestry nor the product of either Queen Matilda's hand or design. It is, nevertheless, impressive.

This 70-metre-long, 50-centimetre-wide strip cartoon is a band of linen, embroidered in a trillion stitches of coloured wool made in England (in Kent, actually) by William's half-brother Bishop Odo.

It was brought to Bayeux to decorate the nave of the cathedral on feast days. Each year, half a million people come to the Centre Guillaume-le-Conquérant (housed in one of Bayeux's fine old mansions) to pay their respects, following a tedious, tantalising, circuitous route through a cinema, background displays, various slide presentations, back staircases and fire escapes before coming face to face with the real thing. Which goes on and on and on. If you are confused about who's who, the English are the lads with the moustaches.

There are two lacemaking schools in Bayeux where you can enrol for classes as short as half an hour and be taught to make a small sample of the distinctive Bayeux lace. The Atelier de la Dentelle is in the Hôtel du Doyen, rue Lambert Leforestier, and the Atelier de l'Horloge is in rue de la Poissonnerie.

Hôtel Lion d'Or: Bayeux's star coaching inn, a Logis de France and Relais du Silence, is set back from the road. Its restaurant, open since 1640 and one of the best in Normandy, is particularly popular with visitors from Britain. Thirty rooms overlook a quiet central courtyard, full of red geraniums to match the cheery red bedroom awnings. The décor in the rooms is a little garish but constant refurbishing keeps them comfortable. *Rue St Jean,* ☎ *31 92 06 90. Moderate to expensive.*

Hôtel Notre Dame: an 'all options to all people' Logis de France hotel which has no less than four restaurants. The building's exterior is old, in keeping with Bayeux, but inside it is crisp and modern. The hotel is central, right opposite the cathedral, but the bells may summon you a few more times than you would choose. *Rue des Cuisiniers,* ☎ *31 92 87 24. Inexpensive to moderate.*

Arromanches

The high point in the hitherto uneventful history of this quiet fishing-village-cum-resort at the mouth of the tiny Arro river was its selection in 1944 as the site for the artificial Mulberry Harbour. Today many tourists annually swell the number of its 400 or so inhabitants, especially on the anniversary of D-Day when they climb up to Asnelles to get the best view of the vast remnants of harbour that still float in the bay and to visit the D-Day memorial museum at the eastern end of Arromanches (open every day), whose excellent displays of Royal Navy and American film, artillery remains and other memorabilia, will either tap sentiment or imagination, depending on the generation.

Falaise

Falaise would hold little interest for the tourist were it not for the fact that William the Conqueror was born here. However, the town is superbly situated in a gorge of the river Ante, crowned by an immense, moody castle, built by William's ancestors, and dominating a rocky spur above the valley. The castle was lucky enough to survive heavy air attacks in the summer of 1944 when two-thirds of Falaise was completely laid waste. You can now walk around the ramparts, pay homage to William's statue at the foot of the castle, and visit the large, rectangular and very cold twelfth-century dungeon.

Courseulles

This little town's claim to fame came when, on 12 June 1944, Winston Churchill landed here, closely followed by Général de Gaulle and King George VI. However, apart from a Sherman tank which was dredged up from the sea and which now stands in the middle of town, and the granite monument near the beach to commemorate de Gaulle's landing, you could easily remain unaware of Courseulles' wartime links. Tall, modern grey-and-white buildings – mainly apartments and hotels – loom large: evidence of its prosperity as a tourist resort with its huge yachting harbour and fisheries (Breton and Portuguese oysters are transported from the Ile de Ré to mature in Courseulles' oyster beds – from where you can buy them direct).

The D-Day Landing Beaches

During the Hundred Years' War the proximity of Normandy's many fine beaches to the English Coast made them the obvious choice for uninvited guests. The first was Edward III in 1346, and from then until the Battle of Formigny in 1450 Normandy was an almost perpetual battlefield. After its reconquest by the French kings, the area remained relatively quiet until June 1940 when the whole of Normandy was occupied by the Germans. On 6 June 1944 a twentieth-century armada crossed the Channel, the D-Day military operation that allowed the Allies to gain a foothold in France and eventual victory in Europe. The landing beaches and Dropping Zones fall, for the most part, in Calvados (although Utah Beach is in nearby Manche – see Cherbourg, p. 69).

When you arrive by ferry in Ouistreham you are virtually on Sword Beach, landing spot for the 3rd British Infantry Division whose mission was to take Caen. From here, drive along the Côte de Nacre and you pass Juno, landing spot for the Canadians, and Gold beaches, on the way to Arromanches. Continue to Longues, with its immaculate German gun emplacement and on to Port-en-Bassin where, if it's Sunday morning, you'll catch the fresh fish market. You can either turn back here, returning via Bayeux, or continue along the coast to the American landing beaches, Omaha and Utah, the only ones to retain their code names. One of the most difficult of all the landings was on Omaha, where the 1st US Infantry Division suffered heavy losses.

A Bus Vert tour of the landing beaches leaves Caen's bus station on Monday and Wednesday mornings during the summer, calling at various resorts along the coast: spend the morning in Arromanches, lunch in Ryes, and potter around Omaha Beach, Pointe du Hoc, Grandcamp (a small fishing port), and Bayeux all afternoon, returning to Caen in the early evening.

Route du Fromage

Following a rough triangle between Caen, Falaise and Livarot, this route covers the area known as the Pays d'Auge, whose farm and factory *fromageries* produce the four regional cheeses: Livarot, Pont l'Evêque, Pavé d'Auge and Camembert. The circuit is clearly signposted 'La Route du Fromage', and there are four main points of access: at Livarot by the D579, by the D4 from Orbec, by the D511 Lisieux–Falaise road out of St Pierre-sur-Dives, and by the D16. If you visit a *fromagerie* you nearly always have the option to buy fresh, newly ripened cheese, or you can enjoy a proper tasting session before buying at the cheese-making school in Livarot, a picturesque little town on the banks of the river Vire. The route also takes in Vimoutiers, the capital of Camembert where, in front of the nineteenth-century neo-Gothic church in the town centre, there stands a statue of Marie Harel, the farmer's wife who invented the cheese Camembert.

Dukes of Normandy Route

If you plan to visit all the châteaux, manor houses and castles connected in some way with past rulers of Normandy, your route will take you beyond the borders of the Calvados region, as far east as Honfleur. Buildings along the route include the Château de Canon, an eighteenth-century Italian-style mansion built and landscaped by a friend of Voltaire, J-B Elie de Beaumont. Hidden in the vast grounds are the Chartreuses, a succession of interesting 'gardens within gardens', each separated by a wall, and overflowing with flowers.

At St Pierre-sur-Dives is an abbey church built in 1012 by Countess Lesceline (William the Conqueror's aunt) but rebuilt so often since that its original state is now unrecognisable, and the eleventh-century Crêvecoeur-en-Auge Castle is a four-towered building built as a keep overlooking The King's Way which passed through Cambremer. While in Crêvecoeur visit the Schlumberger Oil Research Museum built to commemorate two French pioneers, Conrad and Marcel Schlumberger. Also try to include the park, gardens and ruins of the Château d'Harcourt, west of Falaise, its 70 hectares of land stretching along the banks of the river Orne in a magnificent profusion of colourful flowers and shrubs.

Cider Route

According to the tourist office pamphlet, 'as the cider varies from place to place, it is advisable to taste it each time'. So follow the apple and arrow emblems along the lanes bordered with high hedgerow canopies until they begin to blur. The route explores the apple orchard country of the Pays d'Auge east of Caen. You can actually visit those farms that display a green-and-white 'Cru de Cambremer' sign and see the old cider presses, sample cider or Calvados and usually take away armfuls of farm produce. The route links the country towns of Cambremer, Beuvron-en-Auge, Bonnebosq and Beaufour-Druval.

Calais

For years Dover to Calais was synonymous with crossing the Channel. In the early years of the nineteenth century the steam packet that plied between the two ports was the only regular link, not only for travellers between Britain and France but for the entire European continent. Today it is still the shortest, quickest, most frequent and busiest of the cross-Channel services and, because of its popularity, Calais has become France's largest passenger port.

Consequently, Calais is the obvious choice for a day-trip, a short break or simply a gateway port to destinations further afield. Last year more than eight million people passed through the port of Calais, making the town the most popular destination in the entire world for the British tourist. It also carries the responsibility of being the first taste of 'foreign shores' for many British travellers.

If you look back on the town's history, even the first-time tripper should have every reason to feel at home. Once upon a not-too-distant time, Calais was a British town; it was captured in 1347 and subsequently ruled by Edward III, and Tudor Queen Mary once declared: 'When I am dead and opened, you shall find Calais lying in my heart.' It was also lacemakers from Nottingham who started the town's lace industry in the early nineteenth century. The colonisation lasted just over two hundred years but a few relics remain, which, when combined with the millions of visitors and also the number of British firms now established in Calais, make it still the most Anglicised of French towns.

It could be argued that Calais has become just a little too used to the English. We came across a couple of shopkeepers who could barely manage a scowl and a growl to our polite Bonjour, monsieur or madame (the right and proper greeting according to lesson one in how to get by in France), and there was even one lady who asked us whether we intended to buy anything before letting us across her precious threshold. It's almost as if they sometimes despise their dependency on we foreigners, although, in fairness to Calais, because of its easy access the town does tend to attract the unacceptable face of task-force shoppers who are abrasive with the locals and even more loutish when drunk.

But, despite the wartime bombing which destroyed most of its historic heart, and this more recent invasion of the port, Calais is still France and the charms it may have lost through its celebrity are certainly made up for by its doorstep location.

Do Not Miss

Although allied bombers laid waste its medieval charms, many of Calais' older buildings and monuments cleverly (some say miraculously) managed to avoid the onslaught. Among the most imposing is the town's oldest building, the thirteenth-century **Tour du Guet** (watchtower) which presides over place d'Armes, the main square. It was originally constructed in order to keep an eye on shipping movements in the Channel but since it is now closed to the public the tower can no longer offer the same perspective (Calais doesn't want its visitors to feel nostalgic about the white cliffs).

The **town hall** was built in the early part of the present century in an over-the-top, red-brick gâteaux Flemish Renaissance style. Worth a visit to see the stained-glass windows on the staircase and a painting in the council chamber showing Edward III's capture of the town, it is without doubt Calais' most impressive building. On the opposite side of the street there is a delightful park, **Parc Richelieu**, which offers either a walk, a picnic venue or a slice of recent history inside its **War Museum**, located in one of the German bunkers that was used as the German Navy's main telephone exchange in northern France.

Calais' most famous monument, standing in the front garden of the town hall – and clearly the most popular gathering spot in town for local pigeons – is Rodin's **six burghers statue** recording the sacrifice made by six brave citizens in 1347 to prevent the massacre of the population by our own Edward III. Their lives were spared after intervention by Edward's queen – but Edward still insisted that they were led barefoot, with a noose around their necks, bringing the keys of the town and the castle, to beg for his mercy.

Rodin's studies and models for the statue are on display in the town's museum – the **Musée des Beaux Arts et de la Dentelle** – in rue Richelieu. The museum is housed in a new building and contains paintings that survived a Second World War fire in 1940, and a lace museum that illustrates the history of lace since the sixteenth century, a craft that was responsible for Calais' wealth and fame in the nineteenth century. The collection is the best in Europe, with an estimated 300,000 items illustrating not only local production but also that of the big lacemaking centres of Coudray, Lyon, Plauen and Ste Gall. The museum also houses an important collection of drawings, watercolours and engravings, a series of rooms depicting the history of Calais from its origins to the present day, a collection of nineteenth- and twentieth-century French sculptures and paintings from the Dutch and Flemish schools.

The **church of Notre Dame**, the only example of English Tudor style to be found on the European mainland, is worth a closer inspection (Trivial Pursuit fanatics may be interested to know that in 1921 Charles de Gaulle married a local lass here).

The St Pierre district was created in 1816 when the Nottingham weavers introduced the lace industry to Calais. It comprises narrow cobbled streets and period buildings, located to the south of the town hall, and is the nearest Calais comes to having an old town.

Shopping Spree

More than one million annual day-trippers from Britain can vouch for Calais' shopping potential. Although the shops are not situated near the port you do not have to walk from the ferry; there is a free bus service, linking up with the ship timetables, some to the place d'Armes, others to the central station (return buses leave 45 minutes before the scheduled departure times).

The town has two shopping cores: the place d'Armes, in the hub of the northern part of town and feeding into the rue Royale; and the northern end of boulevard Jacquard just beyond the town hall and as far as, then along, boulevard LaFayette (be warned, it's all a little confusing the first time, especially since rue Royale decides to change its name to boulevard Jacquard just by the railway station). Most British shoppers tend to congregate in the place d'Armes and rue Royale so if you want to lose your compatriots for a while, head south as far as a brisk twenty-minute walk can take you.

La Maison du Fromage: for a selection of 200 whiffy cheeses. *Rue A. Gerschel.*

Au Royal Chocolat: Mme Marie-José Bée dispenses Belgian Leonidas chocolates, the only serious contenders for the title of world-champion choc. Filled with fresh cream and in need of one-per-day rationing. She also sells *délices de Calais*, little chocolate cakes. *Rue Royale.*

Roland Cousin: the only challenger for the title, Roland Cousin is a self-confessed *chocolatier*, pâtissier, *confiseur* and *glacier* selling tiny cakes, expensive home-made chocolates (be sure to leave the price on if they are a present), boxes of petits fours and, something you've long been looking for, preserved cherries in glass boots. *Rue Royale.*

René Classe: selling what they describe as *Arts de la Table*, and what we would describe as china figurines, crystal glass goblets, painted plates, modern cutlery with colourful handles, Christofle china, Kosta Boda smoked glass vases and hundreds of other table-top items. Things that you wouldn't put on the table include wooden seagull mobiles, Christian Dior bags and scarves, belts, and a few items of exclusive jewellery. A friendly shop worth a close inspection. *Rue Royale.*

La Madrague: the criterion of what gets sold here seems to be prettiness rather than any functional consideration. The stock ranges from baby clothes to bowls, dressing gowns to ceramics, glass lamps to candles. *Rue Royale (on the corner of rue Jean de Vienne).*

La Vaissellerie, otherwise known as **Shop-Ping:** everything for the undiscerning tourist, this is a vast emporium of souvenirs, huge coffee cups in all colours, old-fashioned perfume atomisers, soft toys, souvenir Eiffel Towers, wooden clogs for wearing or putting your plants in, 'exotic wood' things, Breton dolls, inexpensive jewellery, cheese dishes and so on and so on, with almost everything bearing the Calais stamp. *Rue Royale.*

Aux Sphinx: Moroccan bags and leather goods galore, from the tiniest wallets to soft-leather suitcases, minuscule manicure sets to compartmented briefcases. Great window display. *Rue Royale.*

Rodier pour Hommes: singing colours as well as more subtle shades of men's clothing, mostly bearing the well-known Rodier label. *Rue Royale.*

Descamps: luxurious towels, bed linens, tablecloths, magnificently coloured towelling dressing gowns, linen sheets, toilet and cosmetic bags and other bed and bathroom accessories. If you miss it in Calais there's one in Sloane Street but since many of the products are locally made they tend to be less expensive in Calais. *Rue Royale.*

Cuir et Peaux: fashionable leather clothes – skirts, trousers and jackets – mostly for women, some in colours several dyes away from the original beast. *Rue Royale.*

Coffea: huge jars of freshly roasted coffee that you buy by the kilo in paper bags or in beautiful presentation tins. Honey, biscuits, sweets, china cups and saucers and herbs on sale, too. Their motto? 'Roasters for lovers of coffee'. *Rue Royale.*

Tabac Le Cyrano: lots of tacky but fun souvenirs with Calais written all over, plus newspapers, cold fizzy drinks and the French equivalent of Donald McGill postcards. *Blvd Jacquard.*

Printemps: a branch of the upmarket French chain, stocking a good range of children's clothes, jewellery, bags, scarves, and interesting old-fashioned hats with veils. *Blvd Jacquard.*

Prisunic: opposite Printemps you'll find a branch of the nationwide chain of stores which, in addition to its mainly mundane domestic goods, also sells food and a range of Nicolas wines. It is also open on Sundays from the beginning of June until the end of September. *Blvd Jacquard*.

Henry Martin: fancy yourself in a genuine French beret? They have a full range here, with their own label, plus *gendarme* hats and others all seemingly flying around in the window (though they're actually tied to a fishing line). *Blvd Jacquard*.

Eram: arguably the best shoe shop in town for men, women and children. A wide range and good designs. *Blvd Jacquard*.

Natalys: a branch of the chain of children's clothing stores. Better buys here in terms of both price and design than in England. *Blvd Jacquard*.

Divergence: a smaller selection of shoes than Eram and just for women but generally more exclusive styles and handbags to match. *Blvd Jacquard*.

Cupillard: tops for kitchenware including Le Creuset (in colours not yet available in Britain), fondue sets, copper pots for cooking or adornment and kitchen knives, all housed in an attractive old building. *Corner of rue Charost and blvd Jacquard*.

Le Temps de Vivre: there's more of interest to the visitor than you might imagine from the Ryman-type exterior. Apart from paper-clips and other boring office items you can buy beautiful stationery, French books, English newspapers and international maps. *Blvd Jacquard*.

Port Royal: a classy men's store with a touch of the eccentrics – from the pair of classic columns that define the entrance to the top-hatted aristocratic logo. *Blvd Jacquard (on the corner with blvd LaFayette)*.

Lablanche: a *charcuterie*, usefully open on Sunday mornings for wine, groceries, cold picnic snacks and salads and hot *plat du jour* takeaways (duck à l'orange was the special on the day we called in). *Blvd Jacquard*.

Caves de France: an outlet for Nicolas wines and a more interesting place to buy your allowances than the super or hypermarkets. *Blvd Jacquard*.

Parfumerie Kloé: a spacious haven of smells, with an institute of beauty upstairs. Famous names on the smart presentation stands include Rochas, Lancôme and Drakkar. *Blvd Jacquard.*

Warembourg: expensive gear for the *homme du monde* – Daniel Hechter, Ted Lapidus, Pierre Cardin and others that you first meet nattily arranged in the thoroughly modern window. *Blvd Jacquard.*

Le Cellier: a wine stockist for anyone in search of interesting labels and vintages. *Rue A. Gerschel.*

Croissants Chauds: for *croissants chauds*. *Blvd LaFayette.*

Au Fin Bec: an *épicerie* with cheeses, sausages, pâtés, wines and other tasty temptations. *Blvd LaFayette.*

Petit La Cave: more kitchen hardware. *Blvd LaFayette.*

New Baby: for tiny clothes. *Blvd LaFayette.*

La Tour du Jouet: favourite toyshop in Calais – watch your child doesn't disappear in here and come out dressed as a clown, astronaut, harlequin, French policeman, cowboy, motorcyclist or princess – they specialise in costumes. *Pl. d'Armes.*

Etchola: a huge range of expensive gifts, and 'just looking' is not a phrase that will meet with approval from the owner. *Pl. d'Armes.*

Gro Supermarket: usefully positioned for day-trippers since it minimises the humping of the trolley between the check-out till and the bus back to the ferry. Open until 7.30 p.m. *Pl. d'Armes.*

Calais-Presse: best source of English newspapers. *Pl. d'Armes.*

Au Gourmet: interesting enough to justify a browse as much as a buy – though don't tell them that. Wines, cheeses and general groceries displayed in an old-fashioned French way. *Pl. d'Armes.*

Le Toucan: a museum of a shop, tucked down a side street and full of interesting imports from Latin America, particularly Mexico. Clothing and gifts for those who are pretending they went further on their day-trip than across the Channel. *Rue des 4-Coins.*

Hypermarkets: Le Continent lies roughly four well-signposted kilometres out of town (foot passengers have to either catch a bus from the railway station or take a taxi from the port). A new hypermarket, **Mammouth,** has opened on the road to Boulogne with around thirty individual shops and a restaurant as well as a king-size supermarket.

Early risers will find Calais well endowed with street **markets.** Place Crêvecoeur, off boulevard LaFayette, comes alive on Thursday and Saturday mornings when it hosts a bustling crowd of traders *en plein air*, and on Wednesdays and Saturdays there is an important, mostly covered, market in the rue Charles Ravisse just off the place d'Armes.

A Place to Stay

Calais has plenty of hotels, though most are rather short of character. The first hotels you pass having just regained your landlegs look somewhat drab but the prospects brighten as you approach the town centre.

Le Sauvage: now part of the chain of Europ hotels, this forty-eight-room establishment, scheduled for a complete refurbishment at the time of our visit, is best loved for its formal restaurant, Le Sauvage, which has sadly lost a lot of its old-fashioned ambience in recent cosmetic surgery. The front of the hotel has opened up as a brasserie, Le Bistro, with swift one-plate options and a few outside tables (which are the nearest thing to having lunch at the end of an airport runway). *Rue Royale,* ☎ *21 34 60 05. Moderate.*

Beffroi: a simple, family-run hotel in an uninspiring building just off the place d'Armes, with the kids occasionally manning the desk while their parents attend to urgent matters of state. *Rue André Gerschel,* ☎ *21 34 47 51. Inexpensive to moderate.*

Le George V: recently and thoroughly modernised, this forty-five-room hotel has, thankfully – given its location on the main street –

been well soundproofed. The restaurant, a good one for fish, is all greys and creams offset by copper pans of dried flowers and light pine wood (entrance in rue Duc de Guise). *Rue Royale,* ☎ *21 97 68 00. Moderate to expensive.*

Richelieu: opposite Parc Richelieu, this is one of the town's most attractive hotels, especially from the outside because of its balconies and window-boxes filled with geraniums. There are fifteen rooms, the lucky ones with views over the park, and the owner is a smiling lady with a little dog, who speaks English, German, Italian and Dutch (the lady, that is, though the dog's barks are equally multilingual). *Rue Richelieu,* ☎ *21 34 61 60. Moderate.*

Le Folkestone: essentially a bar-cum-brasserie with rooms and French right down to the owner's handlebar moustache and Gauloise between the lips. Because of the brasserie he prefers *demi-pension* accommodation. *Rue Royale,* ☎ *21 34 63 26. Inexpensive.*

Meurice: a rather austere building that could pass as a police station, but the only three-star hotel in town. Louis XV décor permeates the massive, opulent public rooms full of uncoordinated *objets* and the bedrooms carry décors to such excesses as bedspreads that look like zebras and colours that could clash loud enough to keep you awake at night. Nevertheless the best in town. *Rue Edmond Roche,* ☎ *21 34 57 03. Moderate to expensive.*

Bellevue: on the busy place d'Armes close to the ferry offices, the two-star, forty-two-roomed Bellevue doesn't have a belle view but is modern, clean and happy to have the English, as the huge picture of the Queen and Prince Philip in reception testifies. Private car parking a bonus. *Pl. d'Armes,* ☎ *21 34 53 75. Moderate.*

Cap Hôtel: looking like a beached blue-and-yellow-liveried ocean liner, the Cap is a most unconventional-looking hotel situated near the station, right beside the slip-road to the dual-carriageway perimeter road. It has been newly (1986) acquired by the owners of Le Sauvage so it is not really fair to judge it by its previous track record, and too soon to make assumptions about the new régime. *Quai du Danube,* ☎ *21 96 10 10. Moderate.*

Bristol: the name, as well as Halfacre, the owners' name, is English, but the prices are definitely value-for-money French. In a quiet turning off the busy rue Royale. *Rue du Duc de Guise,* ☎ *21 34 53 24. Inexpensive to moderate.*

And Somewhere to Eat

Le Touquets: a waiter told us that the English have been coming here for a long time but their tastes have changed. They used to be conservative in their choices and always stuck to the menu but they now opt for à la carte and are *plus experimental.* Can it be that the English translations 'frogs' legs', 'oysters number two' and 'sour-krout' sound so appealing? Or is it maybe the couscous, paella and *fruits de mer* specialities? Noisy but nice. *Rue Royale,* ☎ *21 34 64 18. Inexpensive to moderate.*

Au Coq d'Or: its position on the place d'Armes means that the Coq d'Or is highly subscribed with expats but it is surprisingly stylish, with seventeenth-century tapestries on the wall and lace tablecloths, and manages to offer excellent value for money. Especially delicious sorbets, profiteroles and Cointreau soufflé. *Pl. d'Armes,* ☎ *21 34 79 05. Inexpensive.*

A la Côte d'Argent: a seafood restaurant fittingly situated on the seafront, worthy of a mention in dispatches. *Plage de Calais,* ☎ *21 34 68 07. Inexpensive to moderate.*

Le Channel: good food will always be guaranteed in an establishment crammed with local townsfolk: the constantly crowded tables at Le Channel and its open see-in kitchen are its best advertisement. The menu includes everything an average Frenchman and his family would choose, and there is a hectic, impatient brand of service that he would put up with but which is just a little intimidating if you're struggling to make yourself understood. *Blvd de la Résistance,* ☎ *21 34 42 30. Inexpensive to moderate.*

La Duchesse: one of Calais' prettiest houses draped in ivy with pansies in the window boxes and a couple of conifers standing sentry-like outside the entrance. The menu is simple in its options and classy in ingredients. *Rue Duc de Guise,* ☎ *21 97 59 69. Moderate.*

Le Detroit: despite the name it is not a hamburger joint but a worthy competitor to its neighbour Le Channel. Pastel shades of pink, yellow and white décor and mostly fish and steaks. *Blvd de la Résistance,* ☎ *21 34 43 10. Moderate.*

Le Meridien and **La Sirène:** a pair of restaurants; Le Meridien specialises in meat and La Sirène is your best bet for a seafood treat, especially if you can afford the lobster. *Rue de la Mer. Meridien,* ☎ *21 34 34 14. Inexpensive to moderate; La Sirène,* ☎ *21 34 70 70. Moderate.*

Café de Paris: occupies a strategic position at the end of Calais' main street, so the outside tables at this busy café tend to be an oasis for weary British shoppers. Basic snacks only. *Rue Royale. Inexpensive.*

Nuts and Bolts

Not one, not two, but three companies operate services to Dover and Folkestone with free bus links between Calais' port and town. Sealink buses pick up from outside the railway station, Hoverspeed just around the corner (to the right as you look at the station), and Townsend Thoresen from the place d'Armes.

The tourist office is at 12 blvd Clemenceau, ☎ 21 96 62 40.

Around and About

Long neglected by Britons as flat and uninteresting, the countryside around Calais deserves a break. A mini-one at the very least. For a start, billiard table boredom is simply not the essential characteristic of its surrounding scenery. Compared with, say, the East Anglian Fens, the Pas de Calais landscapes roll rather than drift out of sight on ever-receding horizons. There are farms and long-lost villages, traffic-free and winding roads, hidden rivers like the Aa and the Slack, Hansel and Gretel forests at Guines and Tourne-hem and half-timbered *auberges* that manage to turn up just when the tummy begins to rumble. And that's only half the story. Within minutes of leaving Calais you'll meet the first of the miles of empty, fine-sanded beaches where offshore currents raise the water temperature by a couple of degrees above the south coast resorts on the opposite side of the Channel.

The Pas de Calais is the home of *hochepot* (hot pot) and *carbonnade*, a stew of braised beef and dark beer. Huge vegetables abound from the market gardens of St Omer.

Guines

The D127 from Calais parallels a canal as far as the charming town of Guines, a small town which was first noted in record books in the year 807. Nothing dates quite that far back, although the main square, with an attractive old town hall and a frieze of Tom Thumb houses, are the next best historic thing, mostly half asleep but in a high octane mood on market Fridays. The smaller place du Duc de Guise has a bust of the Duc who liberated Guines after 207 years of English occupation. Nearby is the eighteenth-century clock tower built on the old keep of the Château des Comtes.

On the outskirts of town, in the direction of Ardres, a stone marks the site of the Field of the Cloth of Gold, the famous encounter in 1520 between Henry VIII of England – who fell off his horse while jousting, blaming it on the wind (yeah, yeah) – and Francis I of France. Nearby Guines Forest covers a vast 2000 acres, networked by a maze of designated footpaths. The main parking area is at the 'Bois de Ballon' (you'll see a column that marks the landing place of Blanchard and Jeffries who made the first hot-air balloon Channel crossing in 1785).

La Bien Assise: ten out of ten for unusual location here. You'll find Mme Boutoille's restaurant in the former stables and (aptly) piggery of an eighteenth-century country house which is now a farm and a camping site. The dining room is unfancy, with clues to the building's roots including a ceiling latticed with wooden beams, old candelabra and an ancient ladder hung on the end wall. *Guines,* ☎ *21 35 20 77. Inexpensive.*

Sangatte

Just beyond Sangatte, en route to Cap Blanc Nez and Wissant, the scale of the German presence in the area becomes apparent from the sight of three enormous bunkers, all that remain of the gun emplacement used by the Germans during the Second World War to control shipping in the Straits of Dover and to shell Dover itself. Nearby is the abandoned entrance to the first Channel tunnel, dating back to 1881, and a monument to the aviator, Latham, who was French despite an English sounding name, just pipped by Blériot for the title of the first man to fly the Channel.

Ambleteuse

In the estuary of the little river Slack, this is an old family resort with a fortress built, like nearly everything around here, by Vauban. There is a sand and shingle beach, some Roman remains, and agreeable walks up over the dunes to nearby Cap Gris Nez. Ambleteuse has children's amusements, facilities for sailing, tennis and horse-riding. At nearby Audinghen visitors can visit the Musée du Mur de l'Atlantique, a concrete bunker turned war museum with an exhibition devoted to the Atlantic Wall, built by the Germans to frustrate the Allied landings. The local Syndicat d'Initiative produces a handy map, indicating walks and routes for cyclists.

Caps Blanc and Gris Nez

Both Cap Blanc Nez (white nose) and neighbouring Cap Gris Nez (grey nose) are worth visiting. Cap Blanc Nez is a wild, craggy, windswept headland towering above a huge expanse of beach (however many people were on it you'd still feel as though you had it all to yourself). The 450-feet chalk cliffs, especially rich in fossils including giant ammonites, provide perfect views over the Channel. There is also a memorial to the Dover Patrol, the fleet of British minesweepers who kept the Channel free of explosive obstacles during the First World War. The area around here is rich in bird life (including many species that are not established in Britain despite the convenience of the Channel ferries) and has been designated an *espace naturel regional*. Not far from this point, though the precise location is unknown, is Portus Itius, the place from where Julius Caesar set out to capture Britain. Climbing down from Cap Blanc Nez you'll see pock-marked hills caused by Allied bombing.

Cap Gris Nez, further along the coast, is smaller (350 feet) but closer to the British Isles – the closest point of France in fact. Take time to wander along the cliff-top path, which often dips down to secluded coves, and to enjoy lunch at . . .

La Sirène: the sea views from this restaurant, a conspicuous landmark used by Channel swimmers, are enthralling, but when the fish dish of the day arrives, it's eyes down to the plates all round. Lobsters and Sunday lunch go claw in hand. *Cap Gris Nez,* ☎ *21 92 84 09. Inexpensive to moderate.*

Wissant

A small, picturesque seaside resort full of whitewashed buildings with red roofs. It is extremely busy on Sundays, packed with mostly French visitors and echoing to the clamour of church bells. In the Middle Ages, though it's hard to believe, the town had the same port status as Calais. The name Wissant means white sands on account of its superb beach accumulated between the two capes; it is well sheltered and therefore considered one of the few safe bathing spots along the entire coastline.

The immediate vicinity has very tangible connections with the English occupation of the area since it lay within the '*Pale*', meaning fence, which was the last frontier around Calais that separated France and England.

Hôtel Normandy: the half-timbered Normandy is the grandest building in Wissant and the centre of action in town, taking up almost an entire side of place Verdun. The bedrooms at the back overlook a garden which in turn commands a view of the sea. Other perks include private garage parking and a heated swimming pool. *Pl. de Verdun, Wissant,* ☎ *21 35 90 11. Moderate.*

St Omer

The quiet, ancient town of St Omer straddles the border between Artois and Flanders. It is built on rising ground overlooking acres of marshlands criss-crossed by waterways still used by the town's market gardeners for transport, as well as fishermen (out to land a fallen cauliflower or two) and pleasure cruisers. The banks are also lined with painters and graceful herons. The town has a superb Gothic basilica of Notre Dame (on rue de l'Escugarie), dating from the twelfth century and worth visiting for its beautiful sculptures and carvings, the tomb of Omer himself and its sixteenth-century astronomical clock.

St Omer is full of fine, higgledy-piggledy sixteenth- and seventeenth-century merchants' houses, especially around the central Grande Place next to the town hall and a motley collection of cafés and bars. The Fine Arts Museum houses some interesting tapestries, ceramics, mosaics, ivories and Flemish, Dutch and French masterpieces; and the eighteenth-century Hôtel Sandelin, formerly a town house, is a museum of paintings and Delft ceramics. The place to sit and muse is in the lovely public gardens overlooking the old city ramparts where you can look down over the valley and ravine. From St Omer half-hour boat trips are available throughout the summer which pass the fishermen, painters, herons and the Forest of Clairmarais (a good spot for picnicking, with conveniently provided benches and tables).

Hostellerie St Louis: this U-shaped group of coach-house-style gabled buildings, set back from the road in its own gardens, used to be a nursing home, hence its country retreat ambience of utter peace and tranquillity. The hotel is a two-star, recommended by Relais du Silence and Logis de France, and the majority of its fifteen modern bedrooms overlook the front garden. The restaurant is a cosy mixture of original wooden beams, wall candelabra, comfortable leather chairs and pots of plants. *Bollezeele,* ☎ *28 68 81 83. Moderate.*

La Bretagne: resembling a large Georgian town house, not far from the canal, La Bretagne has thirty-three unprepossessing rooms with desks and table lamps like a students' hall of residence. There are two restaurants, the gastronomic half called Le Best (the décor is far less tasteful than the food) and the Maeva grill which sets out to be a jungle of cane chairs and gigantic artificial plants. *Pl. du Vainquai, St Omer,* ☎ *21 38 25 78. Moderate to expensive.*

Ardres

South-east of Calais, Ardres is a pretty little town, its old houses built around its fourteenth-century Gothic church and cobbled Grande Place. Rather too popular for the sake of its own authenticity. Just outside the town is a lake fringed with cafés and a restaurant (La Frégate).

Grand Hôtel Clément: high quality with prices to match, this family-run Relais du Silence is somewhere to savour on a special occasion. ☎ *21 35 40 66. Expensive.*

Cherbourg

On the wall of Cherbourg's tourist office hangs a massive old relief map showing two ocean liners leaving town, one heading across the Channel for Southampton, the other *vers les Amériques*. The Queen, among others, still comes to visit, but the town's role as a port of call for the great transatlantic giants has virtually come to an end. Their place has been taken by cargo ships and less stately ferries annually bringing a million passengers from Britain and Ireland.

Cherbourg sits on the northerly tip of Normandy's Cotentin Peninsula, that stubby thumb of land that pokes up into the Channel to the east of Guernsey and Jersey. The historic town centre lies just a few minutes from the ferry terminal across the harbour swing bridge. Directions to town could not be simpler – turn right as you come to the first set of traffic lights.

Although you're soon on dry land, Cherbourg is still a city built on water; over the years the centre has expanded all around the dockland heart. The sea is everywhere, even lapping the main railway station at the aptly named Criée au Poisson where the local catch is unloaded every day between 5.00 and 7.30 a.m. These basins are mostly the 'territory' of small fishing boats, French naval vessels and the Sealink and Townsend Thoresen ferries. And yachts, for Cherbourg's busy marina is landfall France for hundreds of British sailors en route to the coast of Brittany. They clutter the town like long-lost Smarties in their yellow wellies and orange wet-weather gear, never quite staying long enough to warm up after their crossing.

Away from the dock area are remnants of the older town which, unlike the harbour which was heavily blitzed by the retreating Germans, survived the ravages of war. Many of the buildings date back to the sixteenth and seventeenth centuries and several of the narrow, often cobbled, streets have become pedestrianised for the benefit of shoppers (those that aren't are usually highly congested by today's demanding road traffic). Pretty well everything of interest to the visitor is contained within this compact heart, an island of interest surrounded by the tall structures of post-war Cherbourg.

The history of Cherbourg is a history of the sea and of war. It played a prominent part in the Hundred Years' War. On the death of Charles V in 1380, Cherbourg was the only town in Normandy still in English possession. In 1450, Thomas Kynel landed here, and marched across the Cotentin Peninsula to Bayeux where he was routed in what proved to be the last battle of the War. Caen, and finally Cherbourg, capitulated.

In 1944, the capture of Cherbourg, with its great port, was vital to Montgomery's plan since it left the Americans well placed to clear the whole peninsula. The town offered stubborn resistance, however, and a three-pronged ground attack was necessary, supported by air and naval bombardment. It was eventually taken on 26 June, but since the port was found to be substantially wrecked and mined, it was not until late August that Allied supply ships were able to dock, taking the place of the temporary Mulberry Harbour along the coast at Arromanches.

Do Not Miss

For a birds-eye view of the town and the Cotentin tip, take the steep road to the top of **La Montagne du Roule**. The **war museum** of Fort du Roule is here, displaying its wartime memorabilia – including photographs, documents, armoury, models and a map room – which traces the stages in the 1944–5 Normandy invasion. Alternatively, offshore perspective boat tours of the harbour are available on *La Déesse des Mers*, departing from Pont Tournant every hour or so. Tours last an hour but the commentary, by a local fisherman, is only in French.

The tall and narrow **Eglise Notre Dame du Voeu**, with its two distinctive towers divided by a statue, stands in the charming, peaceful place Notre Dame du Voeu, surrounded by white shuttered houses.

Lurking behind the diamond-cut windows of what was obviously the town's architectural *pièce de moderne résistance* is the **Cultural Centre** with an important collection of the paintings of Jean François Millet who was born in nearby La Hague.

The **theatre**, which occupies one whole side of the place du Général de Gaulle, is a richly sculpted building, a *fin de siècle* gâteau which would perhaps be more comfortably accommodated in the place de l'Opéra in Paris.

The **natural history museum** is mostly devoted to cases of stuffed birds but also houses a fascinating collection of fossils, shells and rare minerals as well as plants and trees galore in the surrounding **parc Emmanuel Liais**, a Kew-like botanic garden in rue de l'Abbaye.

The basilica is the only remaining part of Cherbourg's **castle**, built to defend the town against the English during the Hundred Years' War and later destroyed by Louis XIV on the grounds that, were it to be captured by the English, it would be impossible for the French to reclaim it.

The high spot of Cherbourg nightlife is the **Casino** (*Rue des Tribunaux*, ☎ *33 20 53 35*); it remains open until 4 a.m. for drinking, dancing, cabaret and gambling at *boules*.

Despite Cherbourg's cinematographic connotations, don't let the prospects of bad weather put you off a visit. In fact, when they made *Les Parapluies de Cherbourg* with Catherine Deneuve they had to employ firemen to invoke a wet mood. Having put paid to the town's unfair reputation for excessive rain, it must be said that Cherbourg, unlike many of the Channel ports, is not a town for beaches. Its one and only, **Plage Napoléon**, in front of the statue of the great little man, is now out of bounds because of pollution from visiting yachts but it is, nevertheless, attractive to look at. The nearest good beaches are at Urville-Nacqueville and Bretteville (see p. 85).

Shopping Spree

Cherbourg is an attractive shopping town, worth far longer than the few hours ashore that a day-trip allows. Many of the old shops in rue au Blé and the nearby streets grouped around the fish market have been renovated and this area is the most interesting section from which to start your explorations (and purchases!). On the north side of the main square (place du Général de Gaulle) you'll find a network of mainly pedestrian-only streets, including rue Commerce, rue des Portes, rue des Fosses and rue Grande-Rue, which have more than their fair share of the town's boutiques (rue des Fosses alone has four: Rodé, Bleu Citron, Passion and Manouik). Seekers of that other French necessity, good food – meats, cheeses, wines, bread and cakes – should wander down the rue Grande-Rue which, despite its name, is extremely petite. Best of the charcuteries is Le Poittevin.

Jousset: hams swing from the ceiling, bottled vegetables and olive oil flavoured by herbs from Provence line the shelves, wines fill the bins and jars of home-made fish soup, pâtés and salads cover the counters. *Rue du Château.*

Mace Sports: a sporting goods supermarket with Lacoste, La Hutte and Le Coq Sportif labels, plus equipment and camping gear, at prices that undercut their UK equivalents. *Corner of rues du Château and des Portes.*

Impact: for casual (at least as casual as the French ever are) jeans, sweatshirts and T-shirts, many bearing the popular Naf-Naf label. There's another branch in Le Continent hypermarket. *Rue du Château.*

Coffea: if you don't spot it you will certainly smell the aromas of roasting coffee beans wafting out from this, one of the familiar chain of shops. The coffee is tastier and cheaper than UK sources. *Rue Grande-Rue.*

L'Huillery: an old-fashioned pâtisserie, *glacerie, chocolatier* and *salon de thé* where you can spend pleasant hours perched over a tiny marble table testing the goods (except during mid-June to mid-July when the owners desert their clientele). *Rue Grande-Rue.*

Galerie Jean-Bart: a smart, multi-shop complex with a restaurant upstairs (see below) and a variety of stores below including a self-service *bonbonnière* filled with baskets of brightly coloured sweets. *Rue Maréchal-Foch.*

La Rue Aux Herbes: all the Channel ports have their answer to the Body Shop and here is Cherbourg's. Annie Letourneur's pine-decorated establishment is a breath of freshly scented air in the Galerie Jean-Bart, selling health foods, dried flowers, china gifts, soaps and perfumes. Perfect for browsing as well as buying. *Rue Maréchal-Foch.*

Exclusive: lots of art deco and other finely designed decorative items for the home, including black top-hat ice buckets which you've always wanted but were always afraid to ask for. *Rue au Blé.*

Yolande: when this trendy shop has a sale everyone knows about it, as pop music is tannoyed from speakers up and down the road. The shop has two branches, one very modern and trendy, the other, next-door-but-one, just as modern but more suitable for the older customer. Daniel Hechter, Serge Blécher and Georges Rech are just some of the French labels squeezed in on laden rails, alongside more casual boxer shorts, bow ties, shirts, blouses and skirts. *Rue au Blé.*

Spar: familiar and unimaginative but noteworthy because it is one of the few shops in town open on Sundays. *Rue la Tour Carée.*

La Cave du Roi: proprietor Jacques Fesnien carries a small but selective stock of wines ranging from five-litre plastic *cubiteurs* to prized bottles of ancient Calvados plus a small selection of cheeses and specialities from Périgueux. The only problem may be parking. *Rue la Tour Carée.*

Ballade au Bout des Mers: a young couple who opened this shop in the summer of 1986 sell nautical-theme products that will have an appeal beyond the horizons of visiting yachtsmen. These include dancing sailor musical boxes, ships in bottles made by an old sailor in Cherbourg, leatherbound cruise diaries, Breton woollen hats, scarves, telescopes and 'Bienvenue à bord' doormats. *Rue de l'Union.*

J & C Guerin: a superb example of a species of grocers that have long since become extinct from the high streets of Britain. The shop is oddly circular, its shelves neatly stacked with a little of everything anyone could need (including Pommeau, a local apple-based *apéritif*). Worth a visit for its looks alone, plus the fragrances of coffee, spices and un-pre-packaged produce, and the gentle civility of Monsieur et Madame who have been smiling at their customers for the last fifty years. *Quai de Caligny.*

Maison de la Presse: the main source of English newspapers. *Rue Françoise Lavieille.*

Liliane Burty: Cherbourg has its full quota of designer-clothes shops, and this is one of the best. Colourful, spacious and very expensive, the shop is well-stocked with Liliane Burty's unique dresses and skirts and Lacoste-type shirts. *Rue Albert Mahieu.*

La Calèche: barely larger than the bottles of perfumes it sells, La Calèche nevertheless manages to cram all the well-known brands on to its shelves, including Payot, Dior, Revlon and Bronnley, gift-wrapped too beautifully to even think of undoing. *Cour Marie.*

Aux Agapes: the name means 'a meal between friends' and refers to the teas, fresh herbs, wine, cheese and a carefully chosen selection of groceries, including the Fauchon and Danos Frères brands. Memories of musky aromas and sawdust on the floor come to mind as does the setting: a historic, newly restored corner of town that starred in *Les Parapluies de Cherbourg. Cour Marie.*

Jacques Pernet: an 'own label' man's shop selling an excellent line in shirts and other casuals. *Rue des Portes, Cour Marie.*

La Cuisine d'Aujourd'hui: the town's source of beautiful-looking and functional kitchenware including white porcelain Pillivuyt and Charles Menière knives. *Rue des Portes.*

Printemps: another branch of France's favourite department store. *On the corner of rues des Portes and Maréchal-Foch.*

Nordi: hard on the marina, the Nordi's main role in life is the sale of duty-free perfume to sailors, as well as newspapers, charts and other nautical knick-knacks, while next door La Cambouse provides groceries and wines for departing crews. Usefully open on Sundays. *Port Chantereyne.*

Au Fil de l'Art: a heavily laden gift emporium with painted clay pipes from Brittany, pottery, leather, brass, glass and, most popular with the British, earrings. *Rue de la Paix.*

Alain Yvard: *chocolatier* and *pâtissier*, Monsieur Yvard's counters are loaded with petits fours, chocolates, mousse and Calvados cake and the house specialities – Les Pierres du Pays, which look like tiny roof tiles and taste of nougat and chocolate. Or you can sample in style in the *salon de thé* section, watching your own gluttony in the belle époque gilt-framed mirrors. *Place de la Fontaine.*

Le Continent: Cherbourg's hypermarket lies directly ahead of you as you come off the ferry, a modern and monstrous-looking building that looks more like a bonded warehouse than a home to fine wines, cheeses and other good French things. There is also a self-service restaurant (Presto), pizzeria, café and bar. Open till 10 p.m., closed Sundays. *Quai de l'Entrepôt.*

The open-air **market**, which monopolises the whole of place Général de Gaulle (known colloquially as place Château), every Thursday, is a brilliant exhibition of flowers, fruit, vegetables, chickens, rabbits, cane furniture, cheeses and *charcuterie*. Several more stalls, mostly selling clothes, spill over towards the neighbouring square, the place Divette. On Tuesdays the same square becomes an even more photogenic flower market.

A Place to Stay

When military engineer Vauban fortified Cherbourg more than 300 years ago, he called it 'Tomorrow's Channel Inn'. But Cherbourg cannot, by any stretch of the duvet, be looked upon as a hotel town. There are enough to go round but those at the very bottom of the price range should be given a wide berth – we rejected more hotels here than in any of the other ports.

Mercure: essentially a businessman's hotel, the Mercure stands out like a sore thumb right beside the port, opposite the new yacht harbour. The eighty-one rooms are equipped with colour TV (with English channels), video, direct-dial telephone and mini-bar, and there is free parking. When it opened in 1964 its first guests were the actors and crew of *The Longest Day*, including Zanuck. The Clipper restaurant feels more international than French but the standard of service is impeccable, the view of the sea impressive and the menu surprisingly good value. *Gare Maritime*, ☎ *33 44 01 11. Expensive (plus a 100-franc surcharge for a room with a port view). Restaurant moderate.*

Chantereyne: like the Mercure on the opposite dockside, the newish Chantereyne shares a sentinel position right beside the yacht marina (the raucous chattering of metal halyards against masts is thankfully shuttered out by the double glazing). The nearest thing in Cherbourg to a Crossroads Motel, attracting a business clientele during the week and tourists at weekends. At least half the fifty-one rooms have views over Napoleon's beach, strewn with seaweed and fishermen scavenging for worms. No restaurant. *Port de Plaisance*, ☎ *33 93 02 20. Expensive.*

Torgistorps: although it is named after a Viking chief, the welcome is far from bellicose, especially from Madame's dog who thinks he is going for a drive every time he hears a room key rattle. One of the prettiest buildings in Cherbourg both inside and out. This fourteen-room hotel has a strong individual stamp to the décor, including stuffed buzzards, above-average wallpaper and breakfast cups large enough to swim in. *Pl. de la République*, ☎ *33 93 32 32. Moderate to expensive.*

D'Angleterre: found in a street with nothing to excite the eye, this blandly rendered hotel blends in nicely. It lacks charm, and the twenty-four rooms are rather like prefabricated chalets, but it is cheapish. *Rue Thiers*, ☎ *33 53 70 06. Inexpensive to moderate.*

Du Louvre: a place for sleeping and little else, though its busy-street location in one of Cherbourg's raunchier nightspots may make even this difficult. (If you don't mind not having fresh air there is a buffer of triple glazing to keep out the noise.) Its forty-two rooms are uninspiring but clean and reasonably priced. The reception and breakfast areas are bright and modern and there's free parking below. *Rue Henri-Dunant*, ☎ *33 53 02 28. Moderate.*

Divette: a starless hotel but the best of the cheapies with big rooms and real furniture. Most rooms overlook the square. Run by nice people and a parrot. *Rue Louis-XVI,* ☎ *33 43 21 04. Inexpensive.*

De France: an overwhelmingly French atmosphere, right down to the winding staircase, old-fashioned windows, floral wallpaper and views into other people's bedrooms. Fifty-three simple rooms over four floors (there's a lift), and a separate restaurant across a cobbled courtyard that gives discounts to hotel guests. *Rue Maréchal-Foch,* ☎ *33 53 10 24. Moderate.*

And Somewhere to Eat

Cherbourg is Normandy – home of delicious food, especially if you like your fish served as straight from the sea as can be and don't mind risking an assault on the arteries from the heavy cream and butter sauces which are the basis of the cuisine. Besides crayfish, prawns and salt-marsh-grazed lamb, Normandy is also apple country which means fruit, *tarte aux pommes* and the famous cider and Calvados brandy. Restaurants in Cherbourg itself are not bountiful but they are good and mostly centred in the streets around the old basilica which tends towards the seediest part of town (above all on a Saturday night when fishermen and visiting sailors do most of their drinking).

Café Le Pavé: you could easily miss this tucked-away bar, but since it is one of the few places open for food and live music till 4 a.m. you're certain to hear it. Primarily a bar, open evenings only, with a pub-grub simple menu of vegetable pies, pizzas, quiche, steaks and other grills. *Passage Digard,* ☎ *33 93 53 80. Inexpensive.*

Les Balladins: another hard-to-find bar-plus in the restored quartier. Wood panelling, a nautical theme to the décor, a heavyweight bar worth leaning on and a youthful clientele. Steaks, omelettes and salads served all day. *Rue au Blé,* ☎ *33 53 38 22. Inexpensive.*

Café de Paris: a huge fishing net and tray of live crabs in the window is an unambiguous clue to the principal menu items in this long-standing thirties-décor restaurant, which has a reputation that extends far beyond the city limits. Overlooking the port, its menus include sea snails, *raie beurre noisettes* and lobster (the latter, naturally, is beyond the five-pound boundary). *Quai Caligny,* ☎ *33 43 12 36. Inexpensive to moderate.*

Grangousier: despite the Rabelaisian implications behind the name, the meals in this understated professional restaurant tend to the delicate and are very reasonably priced. A note on the menu saying that the food is always fresh because it is dependent on the fishermen is no idle boast, and all the delicious desserts are home-made. Black bentwood chairs and pink tablecloths, and paintings by local artists displayed for sale in the second dining room, also make this one of the most attractive restaurants in town. *Rue de l'Abbaye,* ☎ *33 53 19 43. Moderate.*

L'Aiguade: a small, half-timbered restaurant in an unprepossessing side street where you can enjoy grilled meats, especially local salt-marsh lamb, as a change from seafood. Huge choice of ice-cream and sorbet desserts including imaginative formulae such as citron and vodka and vanilla with Grand Marnier. *Rue Victor Grignard,* ☎ *33 53 38 23. Moderate.*

Le Nantais: far too easily missed if you are just combing the streets, since it stands a little too high and a little too south for the casual wanderer. Just off a quiet square, presided over by the church of Notre-Dame, Le Nantais specialises in Nantais cuisine which essentially involves cooking in white butter. You can also enjoy river fish such as pike, and even paella (to prior order). Plants, paintings and old-fashioned culinary tools hanging on the wall contribute to a pretty ambience. *Rue Victor Grignard,* ☎ *33 93 11 60. Moderate to expensive.*

Le Plouc: used to be where Le Nantais now stands but has shifted to a busier part of town. Le Plouc, run by the Pains, means slow which, as they produce good food only to order, it sometimes is. Very popular, especially with lunching businessmen, so book. *Rue au Blé,* ☎ *33 53 67 64. Inexpensive to moderate.*

ChanteGrill: a bright, cheerful but rather plasticky restaurant upstairs in the Jean-Bart complex whose menus start with a self-service salad followed by a meat or fish dish and dessert from a central bar. Its popularity has more to do with its adjacent piano bar than its cuisine. *Pl. du Général de Gaulle*, ☎ *33 93 98 20. Inexpensive.*

Crêperie du Port: a notice in the window reassuringly tells visitors that 'we take English monnay' and the menu in English adds to the feeling of confidence if not the feeling of France. Crêpes, *galettes* and the speciality 'La Belle Normande' which means ice-cream flavoured with strawberries, praline and Calvados. *Rue du Port*, ☎ *33 53 04 66. Inexpensive.*

La Bretagne: on the ground floor is a large bar and brasserie and, up on the first floor, a slightly off-the-wall restaurant called Diplodocus which serves fourteen types of grilled meat (nothing prehistoric), as well as seafood, amidst a forest of plastic flowers and bright blue tables. Sociably open until 2 a.m. *Quai de Caligny*, ☎ *33 43 51 80. Inexpensive to moderate.*

La Pêcherie: despite its name La Pêcherie seems to feature more meat than fish dishes and is one of the few in town to include wine – half bottles of Muscadet, no less – on the cheapest menus. *Rue de l'Abbaye*, ☎ *33 53 05 23. Inexpensive to moderate.*

Nuts and Bolts

Both Sealink (from Portsmouth and Weymouth) and Townsend Thoresen (from Portsmouth) regularly serve Cherbourg. There is also a Truckline ferry service from Poole, primarily for lorries but with room for a few cars and passengers. Easy connections by rail (roughly three hours) to Paris, the swiftest being the special boat trains that link with the QEII arrivals. There is a bus service linked to ferry timetables between the terminal and the station on place J. Jaurés.

The easiest, most central parking spaces to find are around the site of the old castle near Napoleon's statue or at Le Continent.

The tourist office is located at 2 quai Alexandre III, ☎ 33 43 52 02.

Around and About

The Cotentin Peninsula, that northern neck of Normandy that juts uncomfortably out into the Channel, is undiscovered holiday land. Bordered on three sides by sea, there are no big cities, no polluting industries, no heavy traffic, superb scenery, good walks, good fishing, long sandy beaches and a multitude of comfortable hotels and fishy restaurants.

Still surprisingly off the tourist track, the Cotentin is often referred to simply as the Cherbourg Peninsula since all roads lead south from by far its biggest town. To the east the coast is peppered with little coastal hamlets and small fishing ports like Barfleur and St Vaast-la-Hougue and the beautiful Val de Saire. To the west the coastline rises to the wuthering heights of the Nez de Jobourg and the moody Cap la Hague before running down through beachy resorts like Barneville-Carteret, Coutainville and Granville, all reaping the benefits of the Gulf Stream, and culminating with the crowds milling around Mont-Saint-Michel.

But if you choose to turn your back on the sea (not difficult in this part of the world), you'll find a fairly even landscape of flood-prone farmlands, patchworked with thick hedges, woody *bocages*, little rose-filled villages like Gatteville, creeper-covered cottages and ancient butter-producing towns like Valognes – you are, after all, in the most important *département* in France for dairy farming.

Château of Tourlaville

About ten minutes east of Cherbourg, just off the D901 to Barfleur, lies the Renaissance Château of Tourlaville set in several acres of formal gardens with sub-tropical species, lakes and waterfalls. This turreted fairy-tale castle is well known in these parts as the scene of a tragic love affair between a brother and a sister, Marguerite and Julien de Ravalet, whose incest eventually led to their execution at the Parisian gallows.

Bricquebec

'Bricque' means bridge, 'Bec' means a small river, and the whole adds up to a tiny provincial town in the heart of the Manche countryside, a good alternative base to Cherbourg, some 20 kilometres due north. Be sure to visit Bricquebec on a Monday when the central square is transformed into a seething mass of cattle, all up for grabs. But from Tuesday to Sunday the main point of interest is the fourteenth-century castle where Queen Victoria stayed in 1857 when she came to open the railway to Caen. Built by the then Duke of Normandy, the castle stands behind an archway off the main square. Inside the walls is a mound topped by an ancient, polygonal keep; by climbing the 160 steps to the top you can claim a magnificent view of the surrounding countryside. The castle is open both to casual visitors and guests. . . .

. . . **Hôtel du Vieux Château:** despite its austere format, the Hardys' hotel – part of the castle and one side of the large courtyard – is extremely popular with families. If you arrive relishing the thought of a long soak in the bath, think again: the bedrooms, like the building, are old, and although they have a refreshing character, creature comforts seem to have been forgone at the expense of authenticity – the bath tubs are tiny, the loo seats won't stay up and the thickness of the walls makes the rooms a little dark and chilly even in the height of summer. Avoid room number 3 whose loo is at the end of the bed with no partition between; better to ask for a room with a view of the courtyard with its flowers and creeper-covered remains.

You dine in medieval, candlelit style with shields, swords and guns held in position by upturned goats' feet lining the walls, but the choices on the menu are far too extensive and the food was a little disappointing. *Cours du Château,* ☎ *33 53 24 49. Moderate.*

Valognes

Pretty enough throughout the eighteenth century to be known as the Versailles of Normandy, this little market town, the former capital of the Cotentin and an important butter-producing centre for the region, is today sadly twentieth-century concrete, having suffered immeasurably from 1944 blastings. Beautiful town houses did survive, though, and are tucked away from the main square; there's also an old cider museum which dispels some of the mysteries surrounding *cidre bouché* in rue du Petit Versailles.

La Chesnaie: M. and Mme Couppey run a small *hall d'accueil* on the road between Valognes and Bricquebec, just outside a tiny village called Yvetot-Bocage, where you can taste and buy such typical Normandy produce as *cidre bouché*, pears, Pommeau and Calvados; they also sell *aquarelles* (water colours) and regional pottery. *Yvetot-Bocage*, ☎ *33 40 17 71*.

Auberge du Terroir: an authentic country inn between Valognes and St Vaast-la-Hougue with modest rooms and open-fire cooking. Open only at weekends except for July and August. *Videcosville*, ☎ *33 54 21 59. Moderate.*

La Glacerie

Not an ice-cream parlour but a village too small to feature on most tourist maps, on the road between the Montagne du Roule and Val de Saire. It looks rather like a mountain retreat because of the valley of the little river Trottebec which runs through it. It was not until the seventeenth and eighteenth centuries that this part of the world became famous for its manufacture of mirrors, including some for the royal family, and a museum containing tools used in their manufacture was opened in 1913, bombed in 1944 and subsequently rebuilt as a little farm museum in 1985. Four rooms display clothes, prehistoric finds, geological exhibits and various memorabilia including faded sepia postcards of the Cotentin.

Barfleur

Situated on the north-eastern tip of the Cotentin, facing Le Havre far across the bay, Barfleur is everyone's favourite fishing port, especially to the hundreds of pleasure yachts that put into port here (the majority from Britain) during the summer months. The town's star role in the history books is as one of the departure points for William the Conqueror's invasion of England on the date that is indelibly inscribed on the minds of every British schoolchild (and, no doubt, also tattooed on the French), and Barfleur served as the main port link to Britain for the next two centuries. Today you can see the seal of the *Mora*, William's hardy vessel, stuck like a limpet to the side of a large rock on the quayside. On a clear day, the Gatteville lighthouse three kilometres up the coast, one of the tallest in France, is also within sight.

St Vaast-la-Hougue

While you're on the eastern side of the Cotentin, continue a few miles south from Barfleur to the tiny fishing village of St Vaast (pronounced St Vaa). Increasingly popular with yachtsmen, the town has just completed the building of a new marina; the rest of the harbour is busy with bobbing fishing boats and a community of cafés and fish restaurants along the harbour – all very travel postery. St Vaast is famous for selling the best oysters in France.

Hôtel France et Fuchsias: the fuchsias climb up the walls, round the balconies of the peaceful rooms and onto the roof. Breakfast is a fulsome and satisfying affair, served in the spotless conservatory, and the proprietors, the Brix, have a nearby farm which supplies the poultry, meat and dairy produce for the excellent dinners (the fish comes from 200 metres away). *Rue Maréchal-Foch,* ☎ *33 54 42 26. Inexpensive to moderate.*

Barneville-Carteret

On the opposite side of the Cotentin, Barneville and Carteret are two family resorts in one, separated by the river Gerfleur, with three crescents of beach, all well sheltered by a headland. Barneville, higher up, has the larger beach (about 40 kilometres of soft white sand), the lion's share of houses and a beautiful eleventh-century church, while Carteret wins in overall prettiness, spread out along a calm estuary. Lobster pots and nets lie strung out along the quay and an air of calm silence prevails; you can hear the sailors' chatter carried from their yacht anchorages across the waters. Carteret also boasts the Beaubigny, a well-known beauty spot on one of the largest sand dunes in Europe. From the Carteret

Gare Maritime, fast boats (forty minutes) cross to Gorey and Jersey (with connections to Guernsey), leaving at roughly half-hour intervals during the day throughout the summer – hence the high proportion of day-trippers.

Hôtel de la Marine: situated on the mouth of the river, this English-speaking hotel has superb views and a locally caught fish cuisine soaked in Normandy flavours to match. The food is accompanied by a sea view. *Carteret,* ☎ *33 53 83 31. Moderate.*

Hôtel de la Plage et du Cap: at the sea-end of the village facing the tiny port and boarding point for the Jersey ferries, this old, creeper-covered Logis de France has fifteen modern rooms, very simply but tastefully decorated. It is worth staying here just for the huge restaurant in the sun-lounge, overlooking the estuary and specialising in both fish and local lamb dishes. Menus vary from the *promotionnel* to the *gastronomique*, and a plaque on the wall denotes the hotel's affiliation to the 'Academy of Arts of the Table'. *Carteret,* ☎ *33 54 86 96. Moderate.*

Cap la Hague

Film director Roman Polanski, banned from England, found the rocky cliffs and sandy beaches of Cap la Hague the nearest equivalent to Hardy's Dorset and chose it for the location of *Tess.* The wild granite coastline of this most north-westerly tip of the Cotentin, its heather-covered moorland landscape carved by twisting valleys, and stark, bluestone cottages, also has a little bit of Ireland and a great deal of Land's End and is one of the most dramatic in the whole of northern France. You will probably want to give the nuclear processing plant at Jobourg a wide berth, but don't skip the Nez de Jobourg (if you can see it for the coach parties), whose cliffs, the highest in France at some 457 feet, offer the best view of the coastline.

Auberge des Grottes: M. Fauve had the foresight to open a little restaurant and tea-room up here and, benefiting from coach parties and solitary hikers alike, is doing very nicely, thank you. So are the prices, but he deserves ten out of ten for innovation, and the

food is hot, filling and appetising. *Nez de Jobourg*, ☎ *33 52 71 44.*
Moderate.

Port Racine

The smallest port in France, with its own customs officer to
welcome visiting yachts from Britain.

Urville-Nacqueville

The nearest beach to Cherbourg suitable for swimming. It's also
worth popping inland here to see the strange cluster of towers,
marking a Dur Ecu manor house at Landemer and the sixteenth-
century ivy-covered remains of the Nacqueville Château open for
the public to view the surrounding floral, manicured gardens
('English lawns', as they put it). There is another beach at Bretteville but the best on the peninsula is Calgran Bay, locally known as
Ninety-Kilometre Beach on account of its continuous, sandy
expanse down the western peninsula coast.

Although most of the famous wartime D-Day beaches lie more
conveniently to Caen, Utah Beach, whose surrounding flat marshes
were a suitable dropping point for American troops, is more easily
accessible from Cherbourg. The Musée du Debarquement here
contains fascinating lifelike dioramas of the landings. Just inland,
the town of Ste Mère Eglise was the first to be liberated in France
and it has an interesting farm museum depicting typical Manche
peasant life at the turn of the century.

Walking tour

The Sentier Tour du Cotentin (otherwise known as the GR223) is
one of the official Sentiers de Grande Randonnée, the network
of long-distance footpaths of France (they cover some 29,000
kilometres (18,000 miles) of waymarked routes divided into
roughly 200 separate though often interlinked footpaths). The
Cotentin tour is an ideal walk for introducing British walkers to the
beauty and variety of the French countryside, and runs from
Barfleur to Avranches, a distance of about 280 kilometres (174
miles). The path is commonly known as the Sentier Douanière, as it

was originally used by coastguards on the lookout for smugglers in the area.

Route des Anglais

The nickname has stuck amongst the Cherbourg inhabitants, thanks to this route's popularity with the British. It runs from Barneville-Carteret to Mont-Saint-Michel, the ideal way of digesting this superb coastline in one, taking in the level dunes of the 'Ninety-Kilometre Beach' en route.

Tour du Val de Saire

A shorter, eastern loop starts at Tourlaville, takes in the port of Barfleur and then swings back along the Val de Saire, a place which inspired the writer René Bazin to describe it as 'the most beautiful smile on earth'. To the west the footpath takes you along the savage, steep and bay-indented coastline of the Cap la Hague and the particularly awesome granite cliffs of the Nez de Jobourg towering above the churning, treacherous waters known to yachtsmen as the Alderney Race, offset by distant views of Guernsey.

Dieppe

Dieppe is the prettiest and Frenchest of all the Channel ports. Its narrow streets and historic houses clustered around the harbour and behind its pebble beach are delightful. The ferries offload their passengers right in the heart of town, right in the heart of France. Just step or drive ashore straight into an *apéritif* at one of the quayside bars or, at the end of the day, polish off your *tarte aux pommes*, swill down a café and Calvados and jump on the departing ferry with just minutes to spare. This major plus of convenience, though, will be slightly eroded when the new ferry terminal, designed to take the next generation of ferries, is constructed on the opposite bank of the harbour, although plans do include a bridge for foot passengers, making the walk to the town centre just a five-minute shuffle.

Port it may be, but Dieppe is also France's oldest resort, popularised in 1824 by the Duchesse de Berry when she first made seabathing a socially acceptable pastime for ladies. The town lies at the end of a route aptly known to many Parisians as the 'road of the sea', and Dieppe has long justifiably billed itself as the *Plage de Paris*. Today the hotels of Dieppe enjoy a year-round occupancy of 70 per cent, a figure that many British seaside hoteliers would give their right arms for.

Dieppe's only real drawback, especially for the day-tripper, is its ocean time from Britain. The Sealink Dieppe ferry from Newhaven takes around four hours, leaving you five hours ashore before the return leg. If the Channel is calm, the ride is fine – in hot weather you could almost imagine yourself on a Mediterranean cruise. In a howling Force 8, however, the ferries can put even the old salts right off their lunch.

But despite the breadth of the Channel at this point, it has never proved too insurmountable a barrier between the English and the Dieppoise. The British, joining forces with the Dutch, sailed to Dieppe and burnt it to the ground in 1694; and during the French Revolution a British shipping company operated a service to carry off fleeing French aristocrats. In the nineteenth and early part of the present century, however, the traffic flow was reversed. Visiting high society considered Dieppe as *the* extremely fashionable place to be. They wallowed in its sea-water baths and gambled in its casino, then the most important in France. They also came to conduct clandestine affairs, the most famous being between King Edward VII and his mistress (he also left his mark in town on place Camille St Saens, in the shape of a pink granite, two-tiered drinking fountain, the upper trough for horses, the lower for dogs). And another group – Sickert, Bonington, Turner, Beardsley, Cotman and other artists – came to paint as Renoir, Degas, Monet and Pissarro had done before them.

Right up until the outbreak of the First World War, many British people came here to retire, especially those drawn from colonial postings and the higher echelons of the civil service. Others sent their daughters to join the community while polishing off their education. In addition to its being considered fashionable, the British were also attracted by the prices, as both houses and everyday living costs were considerably lower than in Britain. While today the disparities are nowhere near as significant, you can still eat, drink and sleep in Dieppe for a fraction of the cost you'd pay for the same pleasures in Britain.

There are two distinct aspects to Dieppe. The port with its arcaded seafront buildings looks little more than a narrow corridor of water – the outbound ferry has to perform an impressive spin round on its axis in order to leave. But ever since the Vikings came and exclaimed 'Dyepp!', the Norse for deep water, it has had a high maritime profile. Between the fifteenth and seventeenth centuries Dieppe was in fact the most important French port. Today, apart from its regular links with Newhaven, Dieppe is the main port for import and export for the surrounding areas and one of the top five fishing ports of France.

Spreading out to the west as far as the castle and an intimidating line of cliffs is a deeply shelving pebble beach backed by a gusty promenade and separated from the main hotels by a broad, ten-acre swathe of grass, a popular play area for children and, for part of every summer, home ground for a circus; the beach is lined with several small kiosks selling everything seasidey from swimwear to sickly snacks. The overall effect is to make one feel a sense of regret that the shoreline on the other side of the Channel didn't manage to hold out a wee while longer against the tide of more crass commercialism.

Do Not Miss

Before the massive fire in 1694, Dieppe's buildings were built almost entirely of wood and it was known as the 'city of carved oak'. When 95 per cent of the town was destroyed in the fire, it took architect and engineer Monsieur Ventabren twenty-five years to rebuild it in a style which, though much appreciated by today's tourist, did not receive quite the same accolades back in the eighteenth century. He was nicknamed Mr Spoiltown and Marshal Vauban told him 'you could have done better, you could not have done worse'. Judge for yourself. His contribution to the good looks of Dieppe is now being appreciated and there are several major surgery projects currently under way, especially around the church of St Jacques and the historic quartier Ste Catherine. They are also at work stripping the concrete rendering to reveal the brickwork of several seafront hotels that were too hastily erected after the war.

The **castle** is the most outlying point of interest, a five or so minute walk from the centre and one of the few things in town that managed to survive the fire of 1694. The Romans were the first to build a fortress on the site, but the present castle dates from the fifteenth century, the north tower and the outer moat wall from the fourteenth. The sheer scale and grand design of the building reflect the fact that the area was one of the richest in France because of the activities of the port and the agriculture of the surrounding region. Today the castle, which has recently been considerably restored, houses a gallery with paintings by Pissarro, Monet, Dufy and other impressionists who came to relish Dieppe's light, plus prints by Braque who spent his last years nearby, and a museum containing maritime objects plus a unique collection of locally made ivory carvings (*see* Route de l'Ivoire, p. 104). In the seventeenth century there were more than 300 ivory carvers in Dieppe. Now there is just one.

On the promenade in **square du Canada** you'll see a memorial commemorating the sixteenth- to eighteenth-century Dieppe explorers of Canada and the memorial to the Canadian forces who lost their lives on 19 August 1942 during the ill-fated landing (above the town there is a war cemetery with the graves of more than 1000 men who were killed on that one day).

St Jacques, Dieppe's religious masterpiece of cathedral proportions, hides behind a beautiful, well-weathered façade, with decorative pinnacles and turrets; it fortunately survived the fire, as did the early fifteenth-century tower (42 metres high). Outside the cathedral on the square are a number of fine wooden statues donated to the Dieppoise by Canadian woodcarvers in 1982 to commemorate the fortieth anniversary of the Allied troops landing.

St Remy, another pre-fire survivor, has a much colder, rather heavy exterior, making it less interesting than St Jacques. Inside is an eighteenth-century organ with a sculpted tribune. The church tower was badly damaged during the Second World War and is currently closed for restoration work.

Les Tourelles, or turrets, between the casino and the Hôtel Présidence are the last remnants of the many sixteenth-century stone-and-flint gates which once opened into the city walls.

Dieppe's **casino** is still one of the biggest in France, open throughout the year on boulevard de Verdun for roulette, boules, baccarat, chemin de fer, blackjack and other ways to lose your hard-earned francs.

It would be impossible to miss the huge, municipal heated **swimming pool, sauna, sports and solarium complex** and its adjoining **Thalassothérapie Centre** where you can get treatment for arthritis and rheumatism. Many of the Dieppe hotels (including the Aguado, the Présidence and the Univers listed below) feature packages that include treatment at the centre, often combined with golf on the clifftop course – not, they say, a place to attach much importance to your handicap. There are a number of tennis courts next door which can be booked through your hotel, but be warned: it costs around 70 francs for two players per hour (interestingly, you can rent a court on your own for half the price).

Finally, go to the Café de Tribuneaux at the top of the Grande Rue, a Dieppe institution whose dark eighteenth-century interior has seen the likes of Monet and Renoir, Whistler and Aubrey Beardsley, and the sad sight of Oscar Wilde in exile.

Shopping Spree

Dieppe, because of its compact network of main streets, is a shoppers' town. The lower half of rue de la Barre is pedestrianised and it leads into the other shopping artery, the Grande Rue (cars are also banned from here). But don't just peer into the shop windows. Most of the buildings have beautiful, wrought-iron balconies built during the town's eighteenth-century restoration.

Mariette: a small but beautiful department store selling toys, household goods, aprons, bags, swimsuits, towels, sunshades, garden furniture and clothes. *Rue de la Barre*.

Printemps: a branch of the nationwide department store; next to but more upmarket than **Prisunic** (to which it is amicably linked). Particularly good for clothes, kitchenware and perfume. *Rue de la Barre*.

Yves St-Brice: Mme Volet has put natural resources to good use, creating different, very delicate-looking jewellery made of bright blue turquoise and ivory. She also sells a jumbled collection of coloured watches, bangles, Hermès scarves, etc. English spoken. *Rue de la Barre*.

H. Divernet: you can rely on M. Divernet's skills as a chef of fine pâtisseries – he is a member of the Association Professionnelle des Maîtres-Pâtissiers, gourmet cooks who meet up periodically to exchange recipes and trade secrets, whose goal is to ensure high standards of pâtisserie throughout France. His shop is filled with racks of tasty sweetmeats, cakes, gâteaux and tarts. He also serves fruity ice creams. *Grande Rue.*

Ma Boutique: the Dieppe outlet for Naf-Naf shirts, Buffalo jeans and casual, inexpensive, colourful apparel. *Grande Rue.*

Prisunic: you could stock up on all the food you need in the basement, and wander upstairs for your basic household items, probably at prices you'll find hard to beat. *Grande Rue.*

La Maison de la Presse: a whole wall of this large newsagent and bookshop is devoted to magazines and newspapers, amongst which you'll find the *Daily Mirror*, the *Sun*, *The Times* and the *Sunday Times*. *Grande Rue.*

Royal Fruits: we picked this out not only because of its magnificent spread of fruit and vegetables and its cheese counter (we are, after all, in Normandy where good natural produce is plentiful!) but also because the fact that a greengrocers can thrive in a prime location of town seems to say a lot about priorities. *Grande Rue.*

Eurieult: a top-class *charcuterie*, with hams, seafood, pastries . . . everything. Absolutely spotless and very cool on the hottest of days. *Grande Rue.*

Palais du Vêtement: not quite as exciting as the name suggests, but nevertheless overflowing with jackets, skirts, raincoats, sports jackets, blouses, T-shirts, etc., etc., for kids and adults. Neither expensive nor over-trendy, but all smacking of French style. *Grande Rue.*

Ratel: tops for chocs, all home-made and delicious. *Grande Rue.*

Libraire Papeterie à la Licorne: why do the French have so much more attractively stocked stationery shops than we do? Here is a classic example, also selling maps, postcards and copies of Michelin to tell you where and what to eat. *Grande Rue.*

Rôtisserie Parisienne: a 1909 photo of the establishment hangs on the wall and the interior has changed little since. There are cheeses laid out on straw mats, freshly roasted chickens, game, home-made pâtés, and a stuffed boar's head to keep an eye on the goings-on. *Grande Rue.*

Aux Caves de France: you can leave your wine shopping until the very last minute, thanks to the convenient location of this shop right beside the ferry. Pick up a price list on your way in and spend the rest of the day or weekend deliberating just how best to maximise your allowance. Discounts on cases and all credit cards will do nicely, thank you. *Quai Henri IV.*

Claude Olivier: the quiet brother of the more flamboyant Philippe in Boulogne can recommend wines to accompany any meal from his cellars of around 350 and advise on which of his 100 varieties of cheese will appeal to your particular palate. He also sells a range of quality coffees and Normandy ciders. *Rue St Jacques.*

Aux Arômes de Provence: aptly named since the sweet smell of potpourri wafts towards you as you enter. Besides baskets of dried flowers you'll find honeys, jams, teas, fragrant sticks for burning in the garden, seaweed shampoo and soaps and large, hessian sacks of French herbs. *Place St Jacques.*

Jean-Luc Beux: the owner – young, eccentric, balding and very friendly – stands in the middle of the shop looking as though he were born in his dirty overalls, surrounded by beautiful clocks of all shapes, sizes and ages, some for sale and some that he has undertaken to mend. *Rue de l'Oranger.*

Atelier du Vannier: one of a scatter of craftsman-type shops and workshops in the historic St Jacques area, this one making and selling traditional wickerwork – cages, cradles, baskets, tall baguette baskets, cots, etc. *Rue Pecquet.*

La Porcelainerie: full of Limoges porcelain. *Rue Vauquelin.*

Hypermarkets: Mammouth is the biggest, reputedly the size of ten tennis courts. It is situated on the road to Rouen, a ten- to fifteen-minute bus ride from the ferry (a bus leaves from outside the tourist office approximately every ten minutes). On Wednesdays and Saturdays, for a supplement on the return day fare, Dieppe Ferries coaches meet both the 7 a.m. and 10 a.m. ferries and run to the hypermarket and back to the port.

A small **market** near the church St Jacques sells fruit and veg on alternate days (except Sundays), and every weekday afternoon a tiny market consisting of a few little stalls is set up in rue de la Barre, selling bags, souvenirs and lace. On Saturday afternoons, in the same spot, you'll find the Hôtel des Ventes stallholders selling junk and antiques. But the main event is on Saturdays, when the area all around St Jacques, spilling over into Grande Rue and rue St Jacques, stages one of the best markets in Normandy. Fishermen and farmers from the environs bring wonderful produce to sell, everything from *moules* to pâtés, fat rabbits to local cheeses (Camembert, Neuchâtel, Livarot and Pont L'Evêque). On the corner of the harbour in a building like a giant concrete scallop shell, a small team of ladies sell all manner of fish off stone slabs, all fresh daily. *Arcades de la Poissonnerie.*

A Place to Stay

Most of the best, and quietest, hotels are along boulevard de Verdun overlooking the grassy *pelouse*, the beach and the sea.

There's no shortage of rooms but, because of their high occupancy rate, you'd be well advised to book, especially in the summer and doubly especially if you want a sea view.

La Présidence: at the castle end of the seafront, this flagship of Dieppe's hotels is a little on the modern and garish side if you're looking for Gallic ambience, but for the businessmen who mostly fill its rooms it is no doubt spot on. Well-equipped rooms, with French and English channels on TV, plus in-house movies. The Verrazanne Bar (named after the sailor who sailed from Dieppe to discover New York) and the Queiros Restaurant (named after the Portuguese explorer who discovered Tahiti) are popular places for hosts entertaining clients. The restaurant is brassy, modern and right on the seafront with views of bodies clambering up to the top of the swimming pool diving board and king-size seagulls landing on the windowsills for an avaricious view of your plate. The food is more international than French – a place to come for a steak or kebab as much as for fish. Eighty-nine rooms, fifty-seven of which face the sea. *Blvd de Verdun,* ☎ *35 84 31 31. Expensive.*

Select: standing like a palace at the top of rue de la Barre, this old building was a private house until the beginning of the twentieth century. It still somehow retains that atmosphere – perhaps because of the pervading smell of polish, the Rupert Bear lounging in the best chair, or the owners' nosy dog. The twenty-five simple rooms are each furnished with excesses such as pink velvet head and footboards on the beds, but the real focal point is the thirties-style bar where, according to Madame, the British 'drink a lot but they are good fun'. *Pl. de la Barre (or rue Toustain),* ☎ *35 84 14 66. Moderate.*

Windsor: a grand, old-fashioned staircase hung with pictures of old liners sets the mood of the Windsor. Here we had the largest room in any of the French Channel ports with seafront views and slightly frayed edges. The staff were very friendly when the car battery decided to take premature retirement. *Blvd de Verdun,* ☎ *35 84 15 23.*

Les Arcades: this wonky old building with rooms to match has long been popular with British visitors, many of whom return year after year to the friendly welcome of the couple who own it. Built in the 1800s, with low beams, narrow stairs and creaking floors to prove it, you come out feeling a contorted wreck. The twenty-seven rooms, half with sea views and some with balconies, are clean but not special, even a little down at heel, with peeling wallpaper and other minor blemishes. They are, however, very cheap, whereas the restaurant is both cheap and very special. Where else in the world could you be waited on by bow-tied waiters and served a four-course meal with mussels to start, trout in butter, a *tranche* of Camembert and apple tart for less than £6? The extensive à la carte also offers good value for money. *Arcades de la Bourse,* ☎ *35 84 14 12. Inexpensive to moderate.*

De la Plage: just one of the many hotels along the seafront, but keeping up with the Joneses quite nicely. Rooms are on the small side but light, airy and comfortable, decorated with pink, flowery wallpaper, with a TV and candlewick bedspreads. *Blvd de Verdun,* ☎ *35 84 18 28. Moderate.*

De l'Univers: a rich and rustic interior dominated by an open wood fire framed by a pair of carved elephants, and collections of copper pans and ceramic teapots (the latter perhaps being the reason for the popularity with British visitors of this three-star hotel). The wood panelled and floored dining room, bedrooms with antique furniture, and wholesome Normandy cooking might also count. *Blvd de Verdun,* ☎ *35 84 12 55. Moderate.*

Aguado: there is not too much French about the Aguado, part of which curiously bridges a road, but the late fifties interior has a stamp all to itself. It is meticulously clean, with its own in-house laundry turning out crisp white sheets every day. The hotel is family run and friendly; the present son-in-charge has vast experience in hotel management in both England and the USA, and the Aguados have just spent a small fortune on a new sleek fishy-theme façade, so you'd better say how nice it looks. In general it works as a cross between a business and tourist hotel. Three stars, no restaurant. *Blvd de Verdun,* ☎ *35 84 27 00. Moderate.*

And Somewhere to Eat

You can step off the ferry in Dieppe and almost straight into an excellent lunch (although the most immediate does happen to be Chinese and not, perhaps, what you're in France for). There are, we suspect, more good value-for-money restaurants here than packed into a similar space anywhere else in France. Restaurants line both quai Henri IV and arcades de la Poissonnerie, the latter named after the fish market just opposite. The thriving fishing industry (Dieppe is one of the top five ports in the country) provides menus here with their most common ingredient. Specialities include *Sole Dieppois, marmite* (a type of bouillabaisse) and scallops. In fact, half the scallops eaten in France come from Dieppe. When Pandy, Dieppe's first experiment with American-style hamburger joints, was established, the Dieppoise were horrified. But it is still standing and doing a roaring trade, even with the British visitors, would you believe?

St Jacques: nineteenth-century décor, pink tablecloths and a discreet, caring brand of service that is succinctly described on the menu: 'If you die of hunger or if you are a bit hungry we shall propose you the whole dishes of the list or simply the dish which pleased you and made you enter.' The one that made us go in was sea bass with fennel. An excellent place. *Rue des Bains, no telephone. Moderate.*

Café Suisse: M. and Mme Janackovic are doing a roaring trade in inexpensive dishes from their Balkan homeland, grilled on a wood fire and all accompanied by Yugoslav and Serbian salads. The décor is cheerful (but not cheap), and some of the white tables and red bentwood chairs are outside under the arcades (facing the port). Other dishes include tongue with piquant sauce, and tripe. *Arcades de la Bourse,* ☎ *35 84 10 69. Moderate.*

La Tourelles: typically French, this no-frills bistro with exceedingly reasonable menus is very popular, so best book in advance. It is situated in one of the prettiest squares in town, the one with King Edward's trough. No particular specialities, but good mussels, salmon, oysters, sole. Attractive exterior, with art deco writing in blue and white. *Rue du Commandant Fayolle,* ☎ *35 84 15 88. Inexpensive to moderate.*

La Marine: nondescript modern setting and a generally unsophisticated air but very good fish, which is surely the right priority. The owner has what the French call a British moustache so see if you can spot him. *Arcades de la Poissonnerie,* ☎ *35 84 17 54. Inexpensive to moderate.*

La Musardière; judging by the prices, which are not cheap but amazing value for what is included in the menu, with at least half a dozen choices in each course, you will wonder how La Musardière manages to make any profit. But try and get in without booking and you'll know how the economics operate. *Quai Henri IV,* ☎ *35 82 94 14. Inexpensive to moderate.*

L'Amorique: another restaurant specialising in seafood, especially shellfish, a fact that becomes apparent almost as soon as you step off the boat and spot the crustacean counter in the front half of the establishment, the wet fish section of the business. *Quai Henri IV,* ☎ *35 84 28 14. Moderate.*

A La Marmite Dieppoise: a variety of five or six fishes cooked in cream and wine, sometimes cider – the authentic *marmite dieppoise* – is the speciality of this restaurant. *Rue St Jean,* ☎ *35 84 24 86. Inexpensive to moderate.*

Nuts and Bolts

The four-hour crossing from Newhaven by Sealink Dieppe Ferries is a plus or a minus. If you're using the port as a gateway, with a long drive to follow (and perhaps a long one before Newhaven) it means a good rest in between stints at the wheel. As proof of the value of this break the Dieppe tourist office proudly relates how Spanish lorry drivers, who were forced to choose alternative crossings during a Dieppe strike, returned as soon as the dispute was settled. The crossing is, of course, particularly advantageous for people living to the west of London. And you also save fuel as well as car and driver wear and tear, and, since tickets for these longer crossings can cost less than the swifter hops, money too. But for day-trips you've really got to love ships, Newhaven, or, of course, Dieppe. The day-return only allows five hours ashore but at least the shops, bars and restaurants are just yards from the boat.

For on-going travellers, Dieppe's location, almost exactly half-way between London and Paris, is appealing (as living proof that it is the most direct route to Paris, just watch the Paris-bound British Airways and Air France jets overhead). Paris lies 186 kilometres, roughly two hours' driving, away; mostly along the autoroute, which begins in Rouen, about forty-five minutes away.

The roads that surround the seafront lawns, incidentally, are the best place to park if you are going to linger in town (and it's free; turn right as you get off the ferry and avoid driving through the town centre).

The tourist office is located on boulevard Général de Gaulle, ☎ 35 84 11 77.

Around and About

A large 'Welcome to Normandy' sign welcomes foot passengers as they amble down the ferry gangway in the centre of Dieppe. But the pleasures of the low, rolling hills of Normandy are only really accessible to those with wheels. Turning inland from the coast you are instantly rewarded with the joys of prime countryside, home to patchy black-and-white or cream-coloured cows, all dining out on lush, dark green grass so deep you can't see their knees. In spring the Normandy apple orchards are a mass of pale pink blossom, in summer the fields are blanketed by golden wheat and in autumn the most magnificent of the Normandy rural sightings are the auburn-tinted beech forests (in particular the famous four: Arques, Croc, Eawy and Eu). And noticeably different in this part of the world are the mirage-like fields of colza, pretty purple flowers grown for their oil, offering an alternative to the more familiar yellow blankets of rape on this side of the Channel.

Because of its proximity and easy autoroute access to Paris you could easily include the French capital in the environs of Dieppe. But even though the capital is no more than two hours away there are plenty of alternative attractions much closer to home. Since the town sits in the middle of the long stretch of chalk cliff coastland, the Côte d'Albâtre, the most practical way to explore the area is to divide it into two, east and west of Dieppe.

Arques-la-Bataille

Inland, just 4 kilometres south-east of Dieppe, you can visit the castle fortress at Arques, built in the eleventh century by the Counts of Arques. Though now only a ruin, with the remains of its high towers fast becoming smothered in ivy, it holds mighty significance for the French; Henry IV-to-be and a force of 7000 men fought a furious battle against the 30,000-strong forces of the Duke of Mayenne. Henry won and became King of France. The town is mostly industrial and uninteresting, but among its historic sites is the sixteenth-century church of Notre-Dame.

Manoir d'Archelles: a small Logis hotel and restaurant half a mile from the castle yet deeply sunk into the countryside and sheltered by the low-slung trees of the Arques forest. A manor house-turned-farm-turned-hotel, the Manoir d'Archelles looks intimidating but isn't. *Martigny, Arques-la-Bataille, ☎ 35 85 50 16. Moderate.*

Criel-sur-Mer

It is worth approaching Criel-sur-Mer along the wide, scenic clifftop route which runs from Dieppe. Once there, drive down through the Yères valley to its coastal team-mate, Criel-Plage, a sunny, seasidey, bucket-and-spade sort of place — a children's paradise wallowing in bygone charm, complete with tiny white changing huts.

Hostellerie de la Vieille Ferme: just a few hundred yards from the beach at Mesnil-Val-Plage stands a low-lying, half-timbered line of farm buildings, offset by lovely gardens dotted with pretty, colourful parasols. The rooms in this two-star hotel are uninspiringly wallpapered (mostly with ubiquitous Gallic brown and orange flowers) with brown and yellow furniture and brown and yellow bedspreads, but most are on the ground floor with the gardens growing to within a few inches of the windowsill. Behind the building is a red clay tennis court for toning up before supper. *Criel-sur-Mer,* ☎ *35 86 72 18. Moderate.*

Le Tréport

Le Tréport is seen at its most spectacular from the clifftop-road perspective before you plunge down to the port. In its heyday it was an important trading place but it was severely burnt by the English in the Hundred Years' War and never fully regained its stature, especially when the river began to silt up. Yesterday's Le Tréport also saw William the Conqueror and his fleet set sail for England. Today it is once more a busy fishing port as well as a holiday spot, with quayside hotels, shops and fish restaurants catering mainly for French visitors. There is a beach, a rather uninspiring band of grey shingle, lined with white bathing huts, and shelving steeply down to the water's edge. The Digue Promenade, which runs behind it, is quite a parade ground of strollers, particularly Parisians, throughout the summer.

Hôtel de Paris: if you like your hotels with character you can't beat this. French as far as the eye can see, the restaurant is well known for its delicious mussels and its lamb raised and grazed on the nearby clifftops. Seventeen rooms in all, the only fault of the Hôtel de Paris is that there are no briny views, despite its proximity to the sea. *Plage d'Ault-Onival,* ☎ *22 60 40 25. Inexpensive.*

Maison de l'Oiseau

The house of birds at Lanchères describes itself as 'more than an exhibition, a true celebration of nature in the Somme estuary'. Apart from seeing plenty of happily alive birds through hides on the reserve there are exhibitions of their stuffed cousins as well as dioramas of Picardy landscapes – cliffs, sand-dunes and estuary lowlands.

Eu

Normandy truly begins in Eu, an elegant, ancient, bustling little town 4 kilometres inland along the river Bresle (which marks Normandy's border with Picardy). You can spend a delightful morning here pottering up and down the winding pedestrianised main street and poking around traditional open-fronted shops selling fruit, vegetables, fish and other fresh regional produce, before exploring the palace with its formal gardens and grounds which reach as far as the surrounding farmlands.

The palace has been rebuilt on the site of the original Eu Castle, venue for William's marriage to the Count of Flanders' daughter Matilda (a scandal of the day, since she was his cousin, which led to the couple's excommunication until they promised to build a couple of abbeys – see Caen, p. 34). In 1475 the whole town was burnt down, and it was not until 1578 that the first palace stone was laid by Henri de Guise. The palace was completed a century later by the Grande Mademoiselle, cousin to Louis XIV, and it became King Louis-Philippe's summer palace; it was here that he received Queen Victoria in 1843, a date that historians consider to be the birth of the 'Entente Cordiale'. Inside is a museum named after the King with collections of furniture, local arts and crafts – unfortunately only some of the collections are now open to the public.

The Forest of Eu, one of Normandy's four ancient forests, extends for some 30 kilometres from Eu to the little town of Aumale between the rivers Bresle and Yères. The beech trees here are huge and shady, the walking easy and small villages, where you can stop for coffee boosters, fairly frequent.

Varengeville

To the west of Dieppe is the lion's share of a 120-kilometre (75-mile) line of imposing white chalk cliffs (the Gallic equivalent of Dover's Whites), known as the Alabaster Coast and broken by some forty lively beaches and resorts, culminating with the magnificently eroded arches and the famous 'hollow needle' at Etretat.

Varengeville, whose charm has been recognised by many great artists, is the first place west worth pausing for. Georges Braque had his studio here (and now lies buried in the cemetery by the lonely little Eglise St-Valery on the cliff edge), Miró spent a good deal of time visiting and Michel Ciry composed a great work here dedicated to solitude and the quest for God. But you don't have to suffer such creative pressures – today's relaxing little village spread out along the coast road 5 kilometres west of Dieppe is there to be enjoyed.

Le Bois des Moutiers is a house designed by English architect Sir Edwin Lutyens in the nineteenth century. The tall, creeper-covered building sits in a sea of sweeping lawns, flowers, shrubs and trees, cedars, rhododendrons, paths and terraces, all landscaped by English gardener and garden designer Gertrude Jekyll. It was built at the request of American Madame Guillaume Mallet, the gardens serving as inspiration for her other love in life, music. There is another, smaller manor house (the Manoir d'Ango), signposted just off the road as you enter Varengeville. In the early sixteenth century it was the country residence and farm of Jehan Ango, Dieppe's Governor and the man responsible for the ports of Rouen, Honfleur and Le Havre. In his spare time he indulged in his passion for doves, and rumour has it that even King François I used to detour to visit his beautiful circular dovecote. The house is unfortunately not open to the public.

One of the nicest ways of seeing this stretch of coastline is to climb up to the first-floor platform of the Ailly lighthouse just off the coast road between Varengeville and Ste Marguerite, from where you have a magnificent view some 65 kilometres in both directions. It is open from 8 a.m. to approximately one hour before the light is due to be lit (they need time to look for the matches).

Hôtel des Sapins: a Logis de France set back from the road surrounded by its own beautifully cared-for lawns. The approach, a semi-circular crunchy gravel drive lined with flagpoles, is rather grand but the building, though formal, is comfortable and every effort is made to make guests feel at home. The gardens are put to good use with cheerful red-and-white coffee tables and tall children's swings, and the restaurant, with its starched white tablecloths and napkins, serves unusual ice-creams flavoured with Benedictine (from Fécamp, see below). *Varengeville-sur-Mer*, ☎ *35 85 11 45. Moderate to expensive.*

St Valéry-en-Caux

This is one of a number of villages (or, more accurately, a small fishing town) near Dieppe known as a *village fleuri* on account of its superb gardens of lovingly cultivated flowers (a special 'flower route' has been devised by the Dieppe tourist office, incorporating them all). St Val, as it is colloquially known, straddles a river, with the two sides of town connected by a drawbridge and, though not nearly as attractive as the *fleuri* label might imply, it has some safe, sandy beaches, and nearby rock formations where boulders have fallen from the cliffs above. It is a popular anchorage spot for yachtsmen, and has a large war cemetery.

Fécamp

A large, busy cod-fishing port that leaves the passing motorist with the impression of ships, sawmills and timber yards and little else by way of instant eye-appeal. However, the famous Benedictine liqueur distillery, signposted off the road to the right as you enter Fécamp from Dieppe, is a favourite stopover for thousands of tourists travelling along the coast road. Founded by Benedictine monks in the fifteenth century, the liqueur making was taken over by Alexander the Great, whose descendants, the Le Grand family, still run the distillery. Twenty-seven different spices are used in the manufacture of Benedictine, and there is a room full of bottles of imitation liqueurs, the attempts by others to try and emulate the unique taste (based on a secret recipe). There is also a collection of paintings (legacies of the monastery). The guide speaks English and the entrance fee includes a welcome drink at the end of the tour.

The eleventh-century St Trinity Abbey is one of the biggest churches in the area and longer than Paris' Notre-Dame. It stands on the site of the infinitely more revered 'Heavenly Gate to Paradise', the original church which contained priceless gold and silver treasures until devastated in a thunderstorm in 1168.

La Marine: perhaps before you sample some of the sweet Benedictine nectar, you should line your stomach at one of the charming quayside fish restaurants. La Marine is a big, brassy, well-thought-of restaurant specialising in fish and shellfish. *Quai Vicomte, ☎ 35 28 15 94. Inexpensive to moderate.*

Etretat

A quiet family resort wedged between the Aval and Amont cliffs. This is a picturesque place where such artists as Boudin, Monet, Matisse, Dufy and Braque spent both working and pleasure hours. Offenbach came here to compose, Maupassant to write, and today Parisian holidaymakers flock here to bask on its beach and use its water-sport and entertainment facilities. Well-known golfers also come to test the town's famous clifftop golf course. Worth visiting are the twelfth-century Gothic Notre Dame Church high up on the cliffs and the monument to two hopeful Etretat fliers, Nungesser and Coli, who tried to cross the Atlantic from the Amont. There's a famous Gothic arch in the Aval known as the Porte d'Aiguille, and a needle rock, which Maupassant compared to 'an elephant plunging its trunk into the sea', rising menacingly 70 metres (200 feet) out of the water; and, at the western end of the bay, the Manneport grotto to which you can walk at low tide. For an even more intimidating view of the needle the more adventurous can take a boat trip along the Alabaster coast, but for the best panorama of the entire coastline drive to the Cap d'Antifer.

Route de l'Ivoire et des Epices

There is only one craftsman still working in Dieppe as an ivory carver, following a tradition that was established when Dieppe's sailors were among the first to bring back tusks along with spices from the west African coast and the Far East. The Dieppe tourist office publishes a small booklet, in French and English, with an itinerary pegged to the history of the trade, taking in the best of both the coast and countryside en route.

Road of the Sea

The route from Dieppe to Paris, the shortest between the capital and the coast, crosses the green pastures of the Pays de Bray and some magnificent forests, in particular the beech forests of Eu, Lyon, Eawy, Arques and Le Hellet.

The best place to break your journey is the spa town of Forges-les-Eaux.

La Bûcherie: near Dieppe, on the way to Rouen, in a tiny village called Les Vertus, this pretty restaurant would serve you well after a morning spent behind a laden trolley in nearby Mammouth. Its high-quality meals are so popular that the restaurant has ceased to advertise; at weekends book well in advance. *Les Vertus,* ☎ *35 84 83 10. Moderate to expensive.*

Dunkirk

Dunkirk was virtually devastated by the Second World War. What is all too apparent for the visitor is that it was rebuilt for commercial slickness rather than aesthetic appeal. One guidebook goes as far as to describe Dunkirk as a place 'for long-distance drivers, not weekend relaxers', which is a measure of its easy autoroute links – established long before the other Channel ports got their motorway act together – to Paris, Belgium and Germany. Some guidebooks to northern France even leave it out altogether and the few that give it a mention rarely toss in any other accolades.

But Dunkirk, for all practical purposes, is really two towns. The one that holds little interest for the tourist is the industrial city and port – it is the third largest in France after Marseilles and Le Havre. True, even within the town you can see cranes, funnels and warehouses on the skyline and through gaps in buildings, but to delete Dunkirk from the list of day-trip or weekend destinations because it leads such a busy, commercial life would be a mistake.

Dunkirk is worth a visit for several good reasons – though you'll find that hard to swallow as the Sally Line ferry docks at the western port, some 13 kilometres outside town in the middle of a pan-flat nowhere landscape of factories, freight trains, billboards, belching chimneys and pylons. As a first impression, Dunkirk fails miserably – but wait a minute. You will have already experienced one of Dunkirk's pluses while still in England. Sally Line, the only ferry company to serve the port (Sealink now only carries freight), leaves from easily reached and hassle-free Ramsgate, better known for its bucket-and-spade visitors than Channel hoppers. Dunkirk also offers comfortable landings, uncluttered by other ships, queues for passport and customs and traffic on the exit roads. And those 13 kilometres into town on swift dual-carriageway take around ten minutes by car, just a little longer on the Sally bus link.

Once in town, if you see somewhere that doesn't quite look like France you won't be mistaken. Dunkirk is Flanders as much as it is France and the Flemish allegiances are obvious, from the style of the buildings to the unpronounceable names of several shops and menu items. The Belgian border, which has never been an accurate, historical dividing line between one distinct culture and its neighbour, is just up the road. Here is a different version, a France without the Gallic airs, surrounded by a countryside of villages that look as foreign to those villages just down the road as they do to a pastoral pocket of Kent.

Despite the war damage, several old buildings have survived including the belfry, the Minck, the old jetty. Originally a small fishing village, called 'Dun' because of the nearby dunes and 'Kirk' because of its church, Dunkirk grew into a small port in the tenth century. It has been successively Flemish, Burgundian, Spanish and even, under Cromwell, English, but it has been French since 1662 when it was bought by Louis XIV from our Charles II. Vauban transformed the harbour and ramparts, maintaining that 'we have here the best site in Europe', and today many of the sailors that cruise across from Britain tie up at a quay built by the great military engineer. The fortress element was later enjoyed by Jean Bart and his corsairs whose legitimate swashbuckling on the high seas, particularly against the Dutch, played a large part in the town's history. The feared and famous pirate became Squadron Commander of the Royal Navy under Louis XIV and is still Dunkirk's number-one hero (his 3-metre bronze statue stands in, not surprisingly, place Jean Bart).

Another superb Dunkirk asset is Malo-les-Bains, part-seaside resort, part-residential section of town, just fifteen minutes' walk from the centre but a world away from the unacceptable face of heavy maritime commerce. To many British soldiers the very mention of Malo will send shudders down the spine because it was on this beach that Operation Dynamo, the massive troop evacuation, took place in May 1940. Such sad and bitter memories aside, Malo today is a delightful spot, with more of a Continental atmosphere than almost any other stretch of beach along the coast. In the summer it is France, or Flanders, in a holiday mood. The broad Digue de Mer promenade, lined with cafés and crêperies, brasseries and restaurants, runs alongside 5 kilometres of fine sandy beach where crowds of French (still very few English) come to sail, windsurf, swim, paddle or lie in the sun. In the winter it is an ideal retreat for a weekend *à deux*, the sort of place where moody film directors come to make definitive films about life.

Louis XIV wrote that 'this town is the loveliest place on earth'. Though even the Dunkirk folk of today may feel such prose is just a shade too purple, it is a fact that many British visitors to Dunkirk, who previously drove straight through the port to Calais or Boulogne when the direct ferries were too full, now stay put in Dunkirk. We don't think it is the loveliest French Channel port on earth but we do feel it deserves a visit.

Do Not Miss

Malo-les-Bains, a fifteen-minute walk east of the town centre, is Dunkirk's trump card. It has a beach as far as the Belgian border at De Panne, and the Digue de Mer – a row of small brasseries and fish restaurants fronted by a row of promenade tables. Away from the beach, Malo is mainly residential. The main square, place Turenne, just behind the seafront, is pleasantly landscaped with lawn and flowerbeds surrounding a tiny bandstand where concerts are held on summer weekends.

The **Kursaal** in Malo is the venue for anything from trade fairs and major conventions to 'Holiday on Ice' and the annual international jazz festival, held every April; there are also the Carnival Balls at Lent, a celebration originally started by fishermen prior to setting off for their long annual voyage to the Newfoundland fishing banks and now a time for processions, costumes, dances, music, masks, nostalgic hymns to Jean Bart and, a curious event, the tossing of smoked herrings from balconies onto the crowds below. The Kursaal used to be known as the casino but since the gambling came to an end most people call it by the new name.

Bang in the centre of town, in the place du Général de Gaulle, the **Museum of Fine Arts** contains several important collections of Flemish and Italian paintings from the seventeenth and eighteenth centuries. Another section is devoted to local history; there is also a permanent collection of local ceramics, and a gallery of naval history which opens out onto a garden. In the basement there is a display of artefacts, souvenirs, documents and a diorama on Dunkirk's part in both World Wars.

The **Leughenaer tower**, one of the town's oldest monuments and part of the original Burgundian fortifications, means, in Flemish, 'liar', because watchmen using it during the Middle Ages as a lookout for approaching enemy shipping often raised false alarms. It is not open to the public.

The **Museum of Contemporary Art**, a modern white marble and rather austere building that stands in the middle of a sculpture garden, is one of the most famous in Europe, containing 700 works of current French art from 1960 to 1980. It is about fifteen minutes from the town centre on avenue des Bains.

Near the beach in Malo Park, on avenue du Casino, the **Aquarium**'s twenty-one tanks are home to specimens from South America, Africa, Asia, the South Sea Islands and, to put you off windsurfing, the Channel.

On the road to Furnes (near the Dunkirk cemetery) stands the **British Memorial**, unveiled by HM Queen Elizabeth the Queen Mother in 1959, in memory of the British expeditionary forces killed during the 1939–40 campaign.

Built in the fifteenth century, still scarred from the First World War and badly burnt in the Second, **St Eloi Church** in rue Clemenceau has had more facelifts than a *Dynasty* star. Jean Bart's tomb is inside and there are several interesting *objets d'art*.

Designed by Louis Cordonnier in 1896, the **town hall**, also in rue Clemenceau and easily spotted by its 75-metre tower, was completely destroyed in 1940 but carefully rebuilt in its original style. The front door is decorated with an equestrian statue of Louis XIV, flanked by local celebrities, and a window in the entrance depicts Jean Bart returning to Dunkirk after his famous victory at Texel.

The belfry opposite St Eloi Church is somewhere between 58 and 60 metres high, depending on which tourist board publication you believe. It is usually called the Tower and was originally built (around 1440) as the steeple of St Eloi Church. The view at the top, attainable after a stiff climb, is worth the palpitations; if you're feeling really lazy use the lift, or read about it in the tourist office on the ground floor.

The old port of Dunkirk is now almost exclusively occupied by fishing boats and yachts, several of them Channel hoppers from Britain. You can take a **boat trip** from the Basin du Commerce on board the *Elsa*, which does four or five trips a day from March to September, with a commentary in English. The route takes you past massive steel works, a new lock, the huge floating docks and the piers where oil tankers are unloaded. Plus ships as tall as office blocks. Departures from place du Minck, Bassin du Commerce ☎ 28 63 47 14.

Shopping Spree

Forty per cent of Dunkirk's 600,000 annual British visitors come just for the day, primarily to shop. And Dunkirk well deserves its shoppers. The main streets are boulevard Alexandre III, rues Clemenceau and Poincaré, and places Marine, Jean Bart and de la République.

Florence: a massively stocked *maroquinerie* leather shop selling a range of handbags, men's purses, briefcases, gloves, belts, wallets and well-known brands of luggage (Samsonite, Delsey, etc.). *Blvd Alexandre III.*

Le Sanglier: below the sign of the wild boar you'll find a superb window display of deli-delicacies: vol-au-vents, chickens cooked before your eyes on a spit, *confits d'oie* (goose legs preserved in fat), stuffed courgettes, moussaka, snails and *flamiche aux poireaux*, Flemish leek tart. A winner with local shoppers, who queue outside with baskets over their arms and lists for fancy supper menus in their hands. Delivered to the door, the dishes are useful for Dunkirk self-caterers, but a *traiteur* to the cause of home-cooked meals. *Blvd Alexandre III.*

A la Havane: a good source of presents for those friends who have everything. Choose from gold Dupont lighters, Mont Blanc pens, watches, ties, Celine silk scarves, as well as a range of tobacco products including expensive cigars stored in their *cave climatisée*. *Blvd Alexandre III*.

PimKie: mass-produced fashions on self-service racks with disco sounds. Spacious but still a very tight squeeze, especially on Saturdays. *Blvd Alexandre III*.

Manon: sells not only the perfumes but all other finishing-touch accessories, such as manicure sets, shaving brushes, razor-blades, scarves and other fineries produced by Hermés, Paco Rabanne, Rochas, Aramis, Chanel, Lancôme, Roger et Gallet and Clarins. *Rue Clemenceau*.

Le Don Miguel: English newspapers, cigarettes, souvenirs and postcards plus the indispensable Jean Bart-adorned plates. *Rue Clemenceau*.

Vert Baudet: a well-stocked emporium of children's clothes. *Rue Clemenceau*.

J. P. Millet: sells the designer end of the range of kitchenware, including fashionably grey Le Creuset casseroles and pans, 'Elef' porcelain, a range of ramekins, crystal goblets and fondue sets. Good ideas for presents and a favourite with friends of brides-to-be who go to buy their choice on the *listes de mariage*. *Rue Poincaré*.

Boulangerie Hossaert: a fuel stop for tired shoppers. Pastries, gâteaux, works-of-art tarts, éclairs, croissants, brioche and delicious *pain-gateau*. *Rue Poincaré*.

Pâtisserie Poulain: the place to buy Dunkirk's speciality biscuits 'les Bernardins de Dunkerque', home-made from brown sugar and cinnamon by local biscuit craftsmen and sold in tins with a hundred and one further uses. The shop also sells ice-cream, Bazenne 'sailor's wife' dolls in traditional costumes, fancy chocolates and earthenware bottles of Genièvre brewed locally by master distillers. *Rue Poincaré*.

La Ferme: big wheels of Dutch cheeses fill the windows; La Ferme specialises in Gouda which may seem a strange thing to buy in France but not when you bear in mind the Flemish undertones.

The shop sells an enormous variety of cheeses, which extends from a normal stock of 200 types to 300 at Christmas. *Rue Poincaré.*

Le Manoir: one of the best *épiceries* in town, where you can buy all things delicious and French that will later prove hard to resist on the boat ride home. *Rue Poincaré.*

Forum: a special shopping centre/mini-market in the town centre that seems to stage a perpetual sale. The goods are not at the summit of quality but they are probably the lowest in price with lots of clothing leftovers from the '3 Suisses' mail-order catalogue. Also useful for household goods and its large self-service restaurant/cafeteria. *Rue de l'Amiral-Ronarc'h.*

Au Brin de Folie: mostly *porcelaine blanche* figurines, crockery, eggcups, ornaments, umbrella stands and vases, plus a small range of glassware. *Rue Thévenet.*

Uniprix: a British Home Stores-type department store in the middle of town and a very good reason for not bothering to go to the hypermarkets. It sells all sorts of products, from clothes to pharmaceuticals, sunglasses to nappies, and an amazingly huge range of hair dyes, but half the store is devoted to fantastic food, including unusual varieties of vegetables, cheeses, wines, etc., all beautifully displayed and reachable without the usual crowds. There's a free car park on the top of the building. *Pl. de la République.*

Les Galeries: next door to Uniprix, the Debenhams of Dunkirk sells everything but food, including sportsware, kitchenware, artificial flowers, perfume, and slightly more upmarket clothing than Uniprix, spread over six floors with a basement. *Corner of pl. de la République and blvd Alexandre III.*

Au Vieux Dunkerque: a small complex of elegant shops mostly selling antiques and works of art in a restored seventeenth-century courtyard, also referred to as the Golden Lion Market. The cobblestones, navy blue shutters, ye olde hand pump, old-fashioned lamps and a background of classical music all combine to provide a touching atmosphere. *Rue Lion d'Or.*

Les Caves du Reuze: a small but interesting wine shop that goes in for special promotions with prices that compete well with the hypermarket offerings. *Rue Jean Jaurès*.

Legros: high state-of-the-art cakes and home-made chocolates, kept in special cases with a thermometer to make sure the temperature is perfect. Take away or take in the *Salon de Thé*. The specialities are *gaufres flamandes*, waffles made locally from pure butter and sold in pretty tins. *Rue Jean Bart*.

Au Fromages de France: a variety of real French cheeses for those who feel cheated by Gouda. *Blvd Ste Barbe*.

Bretagne Marine: a nautical but nice range of Brittany sweaters. *Rue Président Wilson*.

Poissonnerie Turenne: an open-fronted fish shop, curiously decorated with treble clefs and musical notes, selling lobsters (*langouste* and *homard*, which don't seem to have equivalents in the English language), other crustaceans and fish fresh from the morning's unloading at place Minck. *Av Faidherbe, near place Turenne, Malo-les-Bains*.

Hypermarkets: Dunkirk deserves its shoppers if for no other reason than its three hypermarkets. **Auchan** is just outside Dunkirk on the road to the ferry terminal, **Carrefour** is a little further out in St-Pol-sur-Mer and the third, **Cora**, is in one of Dunkirk's suburbs (Coudekerque-Branche). Sally operates free buses to all three as well as to the town centre. As you leave Ramsgate the Sally hostess will ask foot passengers whether they want to go to town or the hypermarket, so have your priorities in mind before you leave home shores.

The huge open **market** on Wednesdays and Saturdays in the place du Général de Gaulle opposite the theatre is a little disappointing for the tourist as the stalls are mostly devoted to clothes and shoes but it's still worth a detour for atmosphere. Because many of the traders are from Tunisia and Algeria it has shades of an African bazaar. There is a smaller market at Petite-Synthe in the western end of town on Thursday mornings on place Louis XIV, fairly near Auchan.

A Place to Stay

Until recent years Dunkirk's hotels catered almost exclusively for businessmen, but as more and more tourists began to discover the port as a place to stay, as opposed to a port to pass through, their weekend trade has blossomed and several now offer weekend packages to tourists.

Le XIX Siècle: occupying an entire corner of place de la Gare with boxes spilling blooms at every window, this nineteenth-century Logis hotel seemed to us the best bet of all Dunkirk's hotels. Full marks to owner Gaetan Badts for his gentle friendliness and superb cooking, with a penchant for offal and the local *Potje Vleesch* casserole. Little wonder he is Vice-President of the Dunkirk Hoteliers and Restaurateurs Association. *Pl. de la Gare,* ☎ *28 66 79 28. Rooms inexpensive to moderate, restaurant moderate.*

L'Hirondelle: one of Dunkirk's two-star establishments in Malo-les-Bains with a modern, cheerful restaurant capable of seating 100 people and with what they proudly refer to as their *cave renommée.* A favourite in-town stopover for reps, which is always a good sign (though the billiard room might have a lot to do with the appeal). *Av. Faidherbe,* ☎ *28 63 17 65. Inexpensive to moderate.*

Frantel: the twenty-two floor, high-rise hotel with 126 rooms overlooks the Bassin de Commerce. It is one of the main business hotels in town and predictably lacks any French atmosphere but the views of the port are superb (the higher the better). *Tour du Reuze,* ☎ *28 59 11 11. Expensive (discounts are available for Sally passengers).*

Borel: a three-star, part of the Inter-Hotel chain, with a useful café and shop selling magazines, cigarettes, newspapers, etc. The restaurant is unfortunately only open for groups, mainly Wallace Arnold coach trippers on a one-night stand on their way back to Britain. *Rue l'Hermite,* ☎ *28 66 51 80. Expensive.*

Eole: spilling out on to the seafront, the one-star Eole has a lot of character and caring touches such as a shelf of books for everyone to use. There's a brasserie as you go in and a pink restaurant upstairs which serves lots of Caribbean specialities with creole sauces on the fish – the chef is from the Dutch Antilles. There's a basement disco, though well-soundproofed from the rest of the hotel, and a video room, but the memorable joy is eating and sleeping with a view of the sea. *Digue de Mer,* ☎ *28 69 13 64. Inexpensive rooms and brasserie, moderate restaurant.*

Familial: a one-star, welcoming establishment on the seafront at Malo, featuring live entertainment for kids (though we were too old to experience it). *Rue de la Digue,* ☎ *28 63 50 05. Inexpensive.*

Europ: fussily modern, this Mapotel three-star with 130 rooms was built in 1970 as a measure of the increased fortunes of the city. It caters primarily for business customers (direct-dial phones, mini-bars, colour TVs in the rooms), and has its own car park. It has two independent restaurants, however. Au Mareyeur is a fish restaurant, with a tank of live specimens (try the Flemish soup *Le Waterzoi*), and attractive wooden furnishing, tiled floors and blue tablecloths. The other, Grill Europ, is more like a pub with lots of heavy wood and exposed brick and an impressive self-service central counter laden with dishes of *hors d'oeuvres. Rue du Leughenaer,* ☎ *28 66 29 07. Expensive.*

Du Berger: ideal for those who prefer to avoid the noise and bustle of the town centre, the Berger stands half a mile from the southern Calais–Belgium bypass road. Big breakfasts, bigger welcome, simple, clean rooms. *Blvd Vauban, Coudekerque-Branche,* ☎ *28 64 94 42. Moderate.*

And Somewhere to Eat

Dunkirk is the only French Channel port where you have a choice of French or Flemish cuisine as well as good fish restaurants.

La Farigoule: we haven't included ethnic restaurants in this book but we make an exception here to include this spotless pizzeria that is so popular with British visitors. It serves other dishes (ham omelettes, pastas, etc.) as well as top-quality pizzas which are baked in a wood-burning oven by owner Claude Calzetta who comes from the South of France and adheres strictly to the

Provençal style of wafer-thin pastry pizzas. *Rue de l'Amiral Ronarc'h*, ☎ *28 59 11 13. Inexpensive.*

Le Petit St Eloi: half-bistro, half-bar with marble tables and a dish of the day chalked up on a blackboard (*coqueville de poisson* on our D-Day). Loaded with atmosphere, with picture-covered walls and tiled floor, the piano you see is no mere ornament: there is live jazz several evenings a week, and the Tarot Club meets every Friday (to play the game, not read fortunes). *Rue Thévenet,* ☎ *28 66 13 13. Inexpensive.*

Au Bon Coin: a nondescript building just behind the seafront in Malo and easily missed if you don't know where you are going. Monsieur Loywyk has owned this top fish restaurant for nearly thirty years, during which time it has been patronised by a gallery of famous people – their autographed photos line the corridors (Philippe Léotard enjoyed 'the best turbot I've ever had in my life'). There are bubbling fish tanks built into the wall and a fishy mural behind the bar. There are also five perfectly comfortable bedrooms equipped with mini-bars and colour TVs. *Av. Kléber, Malo-les-Bains,* ☎ *28 69 12 63. Restaurant inexpensive to moderate. Rooms moderate.*

Le Soubise: situated in the town's most successful restoration project, a group of buildings known as *Au Vieux Dunkerque*. Michel Hazebrouck's gastronomic restaurant is in the historic cellars, surrounded by bare stone walls, and softly lit by table lamps. *Rue du Lion d'Or,* ☎ *28 63 88 55. Moderate to expensive.*

Aux Halles: really a café but also the source of what must be the cheapest meal in town – a daily two-course special with a choice of main course followed by dessert or cheese, plus a glass of beer or wine, all for 25 francs. A popular spot for regulars thrashing out the matters of the day. *Rue de l'Amiral-Ronarc'h,* ☎ *28 66 64 39. Inexpensive.*

Les Paletuviers: on the promenade at Malo, the name of this brasserie-cum-pavement café is that of a tropical tree, and while the Dunkirk temperatures may be a degree or more below those of tropical latitudes, the atmosphere is warm and the menu has a touch of the exotic – every Friday night is 'couscous night'. On other days stick to the seafood, especially the huge platter that includes oysters, crayfish, crab and shrimp. *Digue de Mer,* ☎ *28 63 56 20. Inexpensive.*

Crêperie Breton: though hardly Breton by ownership – Monsieur Barruel is Pied-Noir and his wife comes from Calais – this very friendly establishment, popular with locals, serves the best of Breton crêpes, cooked in full view of the customers. Speciality combinations include honey and nuts, rhubarb and Genièvre (a local liqueur from St Omer) and steak and Roquefort. The menu, in fact, offers whatever combinations you fancy, *mais à vos risques et périls.* Ask for a Kir Breton, a cassis and local cider concoction, but it will have to be accompanied by a crêpe, as the Barruels are not fully licensed. *Digue de Mer,* ☎ *28 63 09 56. Inexpensive.*

La Pelle à Tarte: lots of savoury tarts for starters, such as quiche, onion, etc., followed by a main course of meat or fish, then apple, rhubarb and other tarts for dessert. A neat, newish appearance. *Digue de Mer, no telephone. Inexpensive.*

Café de la Banque: better known simply as 'Le Pub' by both French and British, the latter, one would have thought, being drawn particularly by the Whitbread draught and bottles of Guinness, but, as owner Jean Tiersoone (President of the Dunkirk Hoteliers and Restaurateurs Association) declares, it is the Belgian Stella Artois that the British prefer. Le Pub is just five minutes from the port and is one of the last places to close for the night in town, usually between 1 and 2 a.m. The food – sandwiches, hot dogs and hamburgers – is hardly in the gastronomic league, but at that time in the morning can fill a gap nicely. *Pl. Jean Bart,* ☎ *28 66 65 28. Inexpensive.*

Nuts and Bolts

Dunkirk's proximity to the A25 autoroute to Lille, which links with the A1 to Paris, means that it is a place you can get away from with a minimum of fuss. The Sally Line crossing from Ramsgate takes $2\frac{1}{2}$ hours. Despite the threat of the Tunnel, the port authorities of Dunkirk are sufficiently confident in the Sally route from Ramsgate that they are investing millions of pounds in the construction of a new port terminal which will look more like a modern international air terminal, to be completed in spring 1987. Sally operate buses into town (as well as to the hypermarket) which stop just outside the town's information centre, recently built specifically for ferry passengers. From here the centre of town lies just around the corner. The main tourist office is on the ground floor of the belfry (☎ 28 66 79 21), but in addition there is a smaller office in the Kursaal, open during the summer.

Around and About

Dunkirk's surrounding lowlands are France with a Flemish accent. Although politically you are in France, geographically you are in Flanders, a landscape as flat as far as the eye can see, with barely a molehill to break the monotony. So flat is the area that you won't be the least surprised to spot the 'Altitude 0' sign just outside Bergues.

But though the aptly named Plat Pays may not be the most seductive of landscapes, this lower Flanders maritime plain, reclaimed from the sea in the Middle Ages, contains a wealth of sights to see, from cathedrals to battlefields, and from popular resorts to tiny villages where the inhabitants still speak Flemish. You'll come across sleepy walled towns, with such tongue-twisting names as Zuydcoote and Leffrinckoucke; even new housing estates are crouched low to dodge the wind with characteristic low eaves, red roofs and Flemish gables. The peaceful, pastoral countryside of the Plat Pays is also distinguished by its 'watergangs' – tiny Flemish drainage canals dug to prevent flooding, which criss-cross the countryside and connect with a navigable network that eventually leads to the South of France.

The horizons of the Plat Pays are abruptly boundaried by a ridge of sandy hillocks strung out from west to east, a relatively mountainous 500 feet above sea level. This change in topography has also caused a change in the man-made landscapes. Here you'll meet fortified towns with Flemish names like Watten, Hondschoote and Bergues, and monasteries built on and around hills.

Bergues

The route to Bergues, about 9 kilometres from Dunkirk, is easy – you'll pick up the road signs while still within the city confines. Alternatively, the train from Dunkirk to Paris stops six times a day at Bergues, a mere fifteen-minute ride.

This pretty cobbled town of only 5000 inhabitants was built in the eleventh century on the Mont Vert, the only real high point in maritime Flanders. It grew rich on the textile industry (producing linen, serge and wool) but also produces the strong Bergues cheese, encased in a multi-coloured rind, which tastes a little like Port Salut. Today's quiet town is full of beautiful architecture, with houses built in the Flemish 'birdstep' style, profusely covered in blossoming window-boxes overlooking the Canal du Roy. There's also a tall, fifties-style belfry tower, a typical Flemish symbol of power still flying the Flemish lion flag, built since the war to replace the original which was bombed to the ground in 1944.

You enter Bergues through one of the four gateways in the town's ramparts designed by Vauban, Louis XIV's military architect – his actual instructions, because of Bergues' constant invasions, were to 'surround the city with stones and water', hence the canals. A gentle stroll up Mont Vert will lead you to the shady public gardens of St Winoc, named after the Benedictine abbey on the Groenberg (green mountain) inside – its ruins are now only home to a few pigeons, the walls echoing to the clicks of *pétanque* players on the gravel forecourt.

Other tourist musts here include the Mont-de-Piété museum, an old-fashioned pawnbroker's shop on place Louis Sapelier which now displays Italian, Flemish and Spanish paintings; St Martin's church; a canoe trip on the canal; and an open-air market in place de la République held every Monday morning.

Hôtel/Restaurant Au Tonnelier: Grandmère was sitting out in the cobbled courtyard peeling the potatoes for dinner when we arrived. The hotel, which has been in the same family for more than eighty years, is cool, solid, clean and handsomely higher than its one-star rating. Beyond a bar/café area is the restaurant, comfortably staid, its tables decorated with white linen tablecloths and little vases of carnations, expertly arranged like the hotel window-boxes (Mme Declercq, one of the duo of sisters who run it, has a diploma in flower arranging). Lots of Flemish challenges on the menu – the speciality is a delicious *Potje Vleesch*, a marinade of chicken, veal and pork in spices and herbs, eaten cold with *frites*. The cooking, described by them as *cuisine bourgeoise*, has earned a *Plat du Terroir* symbol, a French national standardisation coding which means there is always a house speciality. *Rue du Mont-de-Piété, Bergues,* ☎ *28 68 70 05. Inexpensive to moderate.*

Hôtel du Commerce: next door to the Au Tonnelier, opposite the church, this is a poor competitor in the character stakes, but is just as friendly. Its twenty-three rooms cater more for the businessman than for the tourist, but you won't be turned away. *Contour de l'Eglise,* ☎ *28 68 60 37. Inexpensive to moderate.*

Le Bois de Chêne: as it was Saturday, their day off, we caught Christian Vandeneeckhoutte and his family loading up the back of a lorry with ice-packed fish and home-cooked gourmet delicacies ready to be delivered to a banquet somewhere out in the country (a common event, according to him). The rest of the week, however, you can sit down to a host of Flemish specialities: fillets of herring, local salad (lettuce, potatoes, herring, egg and tomato), pork cooked in beer with cheese and *Marailles* cheese tart. It is a good example of a restaurant able to combine the best of French and Flemish with produce from the farms of Picardy and the Pas de Calais, close to the Belgian border, which are renowned for leeks, cauliflower, beans, artichokes and other vegetables. The building was completely restored and opened as a restaurant six years ago. *Route de Bergues, Capelle-la-Grande,* ☎ *28 64 21 80. Moderate.*

Hôtel Mercure: just off the A25, 7 kilometres from Dunkirk (between Bergues and Gravelines), the Mercure is everything you would expect from this characterless but functional French chain. Its saving grace is its position in the middle of a bird sanctuary, with a lake on its back-doorstep where windsurfers can do it falling down throughout the summer (the hotel has three boards for guests' use). It also has its own indoor heated swimming pool, car park and restaurant, and sixty-four bedrooms fitted out in typical Mercury luxury. The restaurant is more tastefully decorated (perhaps because the lights are dimmer) and serves out on the

terrace overlooking the lake. *Bordure du Lac, Armbouts Cappel,
Bergues,* ☎ *28 60 70 60. Expensive.*

Gravelines

You'll pass lots of vegetable allotments, impersonal apartment
blocks and Dunkirk's western port along the coast road to
Gravelines. Far from turning a blind eye to the signs to the EDF
Centrale Nucléaire de Gravelines (considered one of the most
powerful in Europe) that looms ahead, 30,000 visitors a year
actually turn off the road to visit the station and the neighbouring
Acquacole, where scientists are trying to breed tropical fish in the
cooling water from the power station. If you want to visit, contact
M. Dumez (☎ 28 23 99 00).

Gravelines became French in only 1658. It was fortified three
times, thanks to Vauban, and you can walk the circumferential
ramparts overlooking the moat. The most important sight to see is
the arsenal, a fortress within a fortress which contains an unusual
art gallery down in the depths of an old gunpowder room (the
entrance is like a tube station and you'll need a pullover on the
warmest of days, but the exhibitions are well lit and worth the
discomfort). Also within the sturdy walls of the arsenal is an
underground bread oven (an ammunition store until 1693) and
the Museum of Engravings and Original Print, with interesting
printing machines, lithographs and other relics on permanent
display.

Gravelines grew in importance in the nineteenth century, when
it was a commercial port for wood and shipbuilding. Today the
commerce and fishing has disappeared, leaving a harbour full of
pleasure craft and yellow-wellied folk. Petit-Fort-Philippe, a
suburb of low-lying fishermen's cottages just to the east of town
and once a haven for all the sailors and port employees, is now a
popular resort with a huge, sandy beach.

Bray-Dunes

This is a tiny village, fronted by a bleak expanse of flat beach and
backed by massive sand dunes covered by spiky marram grass, a
few kilometres east along the coast from Dunkirk. In the winter

there's no one here apart from an occasional walker, jogger, horse-rider and land-yachter, but in the summer it seems as if half of northern France has congregated under rows of sunshades. If you want to amuse the kids send them off on a 'spot the bunker' quest – there are still scores half-buried among the dunes.

Hondschoote

Hondschoote sits on a tiny road to Lille, 20 kilometres from Dunkirk and on the Belgian border. It grew very wealthy very rapidly in the fourteenth century from the export of serge to the Baltic and the Levant. Prosperity lasted until victimisation by a string of disasters – the Reformation, plagues and war – which sent the money-spinning textile industry into decline. There are still a few magnificent buildings left, the most interesting being the town hall, built in Flemish Renaissance style, its entrance hung with elaborate seventeenth-century paintings. Hondschoote also has a beautiful sixteenth-century church, St Vaast, crowned by an almighty spire 82 metres high. And you'll find one of the region's few remaining windmills here, the Noord-Meulen, the date 1127 stamped on its main beam.

Cassel

Cassel sits in the hilliest part of Flanders (once known as the land of windmills) right at the top of Mont Cassel (175 metres high). The city was designed as a point of defence, sitting at the gateway to Interior Flanders. Cassel was the headquarters of Marshal Foch between 1914 and 1915, now marked by his statue in the public gardens right at the top of the hill, and 2000 British soldiers were killed while defending the town in the last war. If you visit Cassel on a clear day, climb up to the *table d'orientation* from which, it is said, you can see five kingdoms: France, Belgium, Holland, England and Heaven! Well, Bruges belfry anyway. Other sites include the seventeenth- and eighteenth-century low, painted-brick houses around the huge, rectangular cobbled Grand Place, and there is a museum of history and folklore.

Bruges

Belgium sits on Dunkirk's back-doorstep, and Bruges is one of the country's finest assets. Just follow the E40 which parallels the canal to the capital of West Flanders which takes its name from the fifty bridges spanning its network of canals. Everything worth seeing is a short walk from the bustling Markt, the central square with its medieval merchants' houses, its ancient Halle (town hall) with its famous soaring belfry and grand clock. Don't be put off by the slight leaning – it's quite safe to climb the 366 steps to the top.

Take a horse-drawn carriage ride, take a trip down Napoleon Canal from one of the landing stages, or simply stroll down one of the narrow arteries and you'll find peaceful squares, gabled houses and still canals overhung with laburnums. The pâtisseries and *charcuteries* are reminiscent of France; the swans, stone bridges and boats may well remind you of the Cambridge Backs; and the canals are memories of Amsterdam. The whole place is confined within four medieval gates that by and large still protect the town from the twentieth century. The most obvious souvenir to take away from Bruges is lace from one of the shops in the Bredelstraat, but you may be tempted by local chocolates, too.

Hôtel/Restaurant Duc de Bourgogne: by far the smartest address in town for transients, this grand old seventeenth-century dame overlooking the canal is extravagant both in décor and the intricacies of its menu (take a dictionary). *Huidenvettersplein 12,* ☎ *050 33 20 38. Expensive.*

Ostend

While in Belgium, despite the confines of this book, it would be a shame to miss Ostend, especially since it will fit neatly into your round-trip to Bruges. The town has a Continental but not really foreign feel to it. The main consumer streets lead off from the Wapenplein, the main square, where there are lots of outdoor parasoled cafés and a bandstand where anything from rock to oompa may be heard. Kapellestraat is the pedestrian-only main drag (home to Leonidas who make the chocolates) while Vlaanderenstraat is a Pigalle-type street, lined with clubs and noisy bars. Rows of seafood stalls line the quayside where you can grab a crab claw, a dish of shrimps, a rollmop or two, mussels, fried fish, oysters (Ostend's speciality) or a nice plate of *warm wulloks* – giant sea snails in a soup stock, extremely ugly but good if you keep your eyes closed. There are several sit-down restaurants along the harbour on Visserskaai; pick one that's serving *waterzooi*, a chicken or fish creamy stew.

Vestiges of War Tour

This is a 65-kilometre tour, easily manageable in a day, which covers all the towns and memorials in the Flanders region that are connected in some way with the First and Second World Wars. Begin at the cenotaph in Gravelines, then take route CD11 to Bourbourg, an important chicory-growing town (you will see the chimneys of its numerous drying sheds silhouetted against the skyline). There are several military graves in the cemetery in Bourbourg's thirteenth-century church.

The tour continues along the CD1 to Watten, stopping en route at Eperlecques in a woody area near the river Aa, famous for the world's largest *blockhauss*. Second World War prisoners were forced to build it as a launching site for V2s on London but it was never used. Tragically, as soon as it was finished, 13,000 tons of concrete was poured onto the prisoners, burying them alive. A V2 Rocket Base Memorial has since been erected by the town.

The route continues on the CD46 and CD226 through Millam to Bollezeele, two villages that contain British soldiers' graves. Esquelbecq, a peaceful little village built around its church and town hall, with a Commonwealth Military Cemetery, straddles the woody boundary between Maritime and Interior Flanders. Stop briefly at Wormhoudt on the CD17 before taking the CD55 to West-Cappel (French tombs in the parish graveyard). Continue to Les Moëres, Ghyvelde, Bray-Dunes and Zuydcoote along the CD60. Return to Dunkirk via Leffrinckoucke where there's a cemetery at Fort-des-Dunes.

Restaurant La Meunerie: arguably the best restaurants in Dunkirk are outside the town, such as La Meunerie at Teteghem which deserves a thousand accolades. The name (meaning 'milling') and the giant, beautifully preserved cogs and wheels in the lounge, betray the building's origins. Each course is a gastronomic experience, introduced to your artistically laid table with a few poetic words by the *maître d'*. The other customers are more likely to be Belgian than French, sensible gourmands who have driven to France for dinner and more specifically for the famous *charriot*, certainly the best dessert trolley we've ever seen. Even the tea was fancy, not served in a cup but in a sorbet. *Rue des Pierres, Teteghem,* ☎ *28 26 14 30/26 01 80. Expensive.*

Le Havre

If you walked west from the rue de Rivoli in Paris, following the right bank of the Seine, passing through rich farming country, the city of Rouen and the Brotonne National Park en route, you would eventually come to Le Havre, sitting hard on the broad river estuary. Napoleon reckoned that Le Havre, Rouen and Paris were 'but a single town of which the Seine is the main street.' But chances are you will come by ferry, across the Channel, probably from Portsmouth but possibly from Rosslare or Cork.

However tragic a situation, there's bound to be someone ready to highlight the superlatives. In 1945 Le Havre won the title of Europe's most war-damaged port; 156 bombing raids resulted in the deaths of 4000 people and the destruction of nearly 10,000 homes. But, unlike St Malo which was painstakingly rebuilt in its previous historic style, Le Havre was transformed into a sleekly modern city.

Based on a chequer-board design, with buildings almost entirely of reinforced concrete, Le Havre obviously has shades of the post-war utilitarian look about it. Architect Auguste Perret, however, succeeded in raising Le Havre well above the drab and dreary by the liberal employment of grand boulevards, tree-lined avenues, manicured lawns, parks, flowerbeds and careful proportioning which is, after all, the healthy respect for the environment that one might reasonably expect from Le Corbusier's former teacher. Add to the blueprint the city's Cultural Centre designed by Oscar

Niemeyer, the father of Brasilia, and you have an architectural experience definitely worth a closer look. You may or may not like what you see but at least shed your prejudices against all things modern before you arrive.

Le Havre is also a relatively new town in an even older sense. After the silting up of the older harbours of Honfleur and Harfleur, the authorities under King François I decided to build a new port in 1517 which they called The Haven of Grace, Le Havre de Grâce. But it was not until the American Civil War, when Confederate cotton, sugar and tobacco were distributed from Le Havre to all parts of Europe, that the port rapidly grew in importance. By the beginning of the twentieth century, when the population had grown to 100,000, Le Havre had become the leading port for American trade and a centre for the cotton and coffee markets. Just before the Second World War its fame was glorified as the home port to the world's largest liner, the *Normandie*.

Today Le Havre ranks as the second most important port in France (first for containers) and the third largest in Europe. With a population of 220,000 it is France's ninth biggest city. Although its days as port of call for the transatlantic liners came to an abrupt end with the last sailing of the *Normandie*, its maritime stature is today accounted for by cargo ships. Its ferry traffic is important but hardly significant by comparison, though the authorities are trying hard to entice more of us over (Mayor Dubois talks of 'daily efforts to increase the throughput, to valorise our image.')

Ninety thousand British visitors come annually to Le Havre, several on yachts (the marina has a capacity for 1600), but mostly on ferries. Many come just to shop, taking advantage of the cheap day-return tickets from Portsmouth, but the majority look upon Le Havre merely as a gateway, taking advantage of its excellent autoroute connections and the two-hour drive away from Paris. Favourite time for the motorists to linger in the city is on their last day while waiting to catch the evening boat home. Since the boat ties up virtually in the centre of town, Le Havre lends itself to a last-minute shop or meal before walking back to the gangplank (if your baguettes are weighing you down, bus number 2 runs between the town centre and the ferry terminal).

Do Not Miss

The main arteries of town are the arcaded rue de Paris, linking with the ferry terminal and known as the city's rue de Rivoli, à la Paris, and Avenue Foch, a Champs Elysées-ish dual-carriageway separated by a central swathe of grass. Both meet at the huge **place de l'Hôtel de Ville**, a central square whose proportions would by no means look lost even in a capital city. It is one of the largest squares in Europe with six ten-storey tower blocks, dominated by the seventeen-storey tower of the **town hall** which, wearing the regulation flag, fountain and flight of steps uniform, forms the hub of Perret's new town.

Le Havre's answer to an old town is the **quartier St François**. Once an island and now connected by two bridges, St François used to be the most beautiful section of town, more recently a seedier sailors' haunt. The **museum** devoted to old Le Havre, housed in two seventeenth- and eighteenth-century houses on rue Jérôme Bellarmato, is the best place to see Le Havre as it was from its foundation to the end of the eighteenth century.

The **port** is an exciting place to visit (other than to arrive in) if you get the slightest buzz out of seeing dockyard doings. During the summer, motorboat tours leave the northern end of the yacht harbour near the beach (quai de la Marine, ☎ 35 42 01 31), and potter round the new tidal basin (with a world record-holding tidal gate spanning 67 metres), built to take king-size merchant ships, tankers and oil carriers. The delightful *Salamandre* boat also operates regular services to Honfleur and Deauville, crossing the estuary of the Seine.

'One day, like this water, the land, the beaches, and the mountains will belong to everyone.' So reads an engraving, in keeping with the town's Communist politics, set in the wall next to a sculpture of Niemeyer's hand, behind the fountain in the concrete pedestrianised area around the **Centre Culturel**. Set in the espace Niemeyer, the main building is locally referred to as the 'yogurt pot' for obvious reasons. It is also a lot easier to say. The Centre is a combination of theatre, cinema, offices and exhibition area (with excellent underground parking).

The **Musée des Beaux Arts André Malraux**, on chaussée John

Kennedy, is built entirely of glass and steel with a 'big eye' sculpture outside on the front lawn and galleries linked on different levels by gangways rather like those on board a ship, a concept in keeping with the maritime essence of Le Havre. The permanent collection includes works by Boudin and Dufy, both locally born lads, and an important collection of Impressionist paintings; the gallery is also used frequently for temporary exhibitions.

Someone called Casimir Delavigne, when looking at the view over the Seine estuary from the suburb of **Ste Adresse**, saw 'Paris and Naples in one picture' and declared that 'after Constantinople there is nothing more beautiful'. Obviously Casimir was born in Le Havre but there's truth in what he said. Ste Adresse is primarily a residential area, ten minutes' walk from the centre on the top of the cliffs which offer grand views across the estuary. Colloquially known as Le Nice Havrais because of its villas, sandy beach and holiday mood, Ste Adresse was originally built to rival Deauville and was once a separate village; the oddest fact of its life is that it was the capital of Belgium during the First World War. Although it has been slowly engulfed by the expansion of Le Havre over the years, it has still managed to retain a delightful, separate atmosphere. There are lots of restaurants and cafés overlooking the beach and the sea.

Walking from Ste Adresse to the town centre along the promenade you pass some surprising beach scenes. This fine arc of small pebbles, broken only by breakwaters and seaweed clumps, runs parallel with Blvd Albert ler, and offers several alternatives to a baguette-and-fromage lunch in the shape of several shanty-looking ethnic cafeteria/snack bar restaurants, such as the Bangkok, the Orient Express and the Hong Kong.

The 700 acres of the **Montgeon Forest** are the lungs of Le Havre. Parkland, formal gardens, forest, a tropical hothouse, two lakes (one for ducks, one for *pédalos*), zoo, horse-riding and sport all flourish within its hilltop boundaries. Here you'll also find the restored **Graville Priory**, dating back to the twelfth century, with a black Virgin standing in the garden(!) and models of ancient houses, manors, farms and more distant archeological finds. There is also a Southampton tree, planted to commemorate Le Havre's twinning with the English port.

Take the two-minute ride on the **funicular** from place Thiers in the centre of town to the top of rue du Docteur Vigne (close by the town-end of the line is a café called Le Funiculaire, ominously named since it marks the spot where the train crashed into the pavement tables several years ago).

The **church of St Joseph** is more than a church. It symbolises the suffering inflicted on the old city from the wartime damage and the emergence of the new. This austere, reinforced-concrete tower that, at 115 metres, is tall enough to be seen from out at sea, looks like a rocket shooting towards the skyline.

Shopping Spree

One of Le Havre's great advantages for shoppers is the lack of traffic jams and the ample central parking space available (the first hour is free in a lot of places). Turn left out of the tourist office and you're in avenue René Coty, by far the busiest shopping street. Rond Pont runs a close second, while the oldest, and at the turn of the century the town's most important avenue, is rue de Paris, where you'll find branches of such number-one fashion chains as Armand Thiéry and Benetton. Place Gambetta is another good place for browsing.

FER7: smart, trendy staff selling smart, trendy clothes – for men only. It has a slightly sporty image: the logo on the business card is a golfer in full swing, with a golf club on most of the shirts, jackets, trousers, shoes, jumpers and flowery, very un-Gallic surfing shorts. *Av. René Coty.*

Printemps: in case you want to buy *all* your presents and souvenirs behind one set of double swing doors, we recommend Printemps on *av. René Coty.* **Monoprix** is further down the street and there is a branch of **Nouvelles Galeries** on *rue de Paris.*

Marie France: her card reads *'le plus grand choix de féminités'*, which in practice translates as very upmarket, expensive, elegant women's clothes: pullovers, jerseys, skirts, etc. *Av. René Coty.*

Bruneau Roche: a master chocolate-maker whose fiery specialities, all made on the premises, are filled with Calvados and

Cointreau (tip your head back or the liqueurs will roll down your clean shirt). The interior of the shop is magnificent, the walls lined with antique library shelves and cabinets bought by M. Boucher from a castle closing-down sale. All selections are packed in elegant boxes which make the chocolates ideal presents. Be careful when buying unpackaged chocolate – in most French *chocolatiers* it is priced in grams, not kilograms. *Av. René Coty.*

Lefèvre: top charcuterie for picnic ingredients including fully prepared dishes. *Pl. Gambetta.*

Abaka: members of staff are like elusive leopards in this shop's jungle of lamps, basketry, white wickerwork, pine furniture and glass tables stacked in piles on the floor like a warehouse, while fragile mobiles hang from the ceiling. *Espace Niemeyer.*

FOG: it would be hard to avoid passing this modern little shop standing temptingly on the corner of rue de Paris and espace Niemeyer as you motor from the ferry port heading south out of Le Havre. Because the stock isn't huge there's room for a spacious display of bright, colourful teenage clothes unusually combined with cane furniture. *Rue de Paris.*

Annette Boutault: the first time we called, Mme Boutault's shop was closed – according to the note on the door, her dog was having a vaccination. But if you're looking for a special present and the dog is home, call in for glasses from Baccarat, Saint Louis crystal and pottery from Limoges. *Rue Bernardin de St-Pierre.*

Mirage Parfumerie: an ultra-smart and colourful perfume house strung out over two levels, the walls hung with framed posters. As well as fragrances from all the well-known French houses, it sells top quality Polo products, canvas bags and satchels. *Rue Jules Siegfried.*

La Porcelaine Blanche: tucked away from the others, it is one of the few shops on the mainly residential approach road to the centre. As the name suggests, it sells the most delicate of teapots, cups, saucers and other decorated porcelain items as well as more sturdy cutlery, breadboards and kitchen jars. *Av. Foch.*

Les Halles: a spotless covered market selling the freshest and best of produce ranging from fresh almonds, fruits from Thailand, *charcuterie*, giant artichokes and flowers. Under the same roof are cheese shops, Nicolas wines, a small supermarket called Unico and a shop called the Ambassade de Bretagne selling Breton sausages, crêpes and cakes. One of the most interesting shops is Cheinisse, which describes itself as La Boutique aux Fromages et Vins de France, not an overstatement when you see the range of products on sale. Best buy is the *vrai fromage artisanale* which comes from specialist farms in Normandy. *Rue Voltaire.*

Normandie Détection: one of the few shops down this street that doesn't sell second-hand clothes. Instead you'll find a plethora of antique postcards, old coins and other ancient Havrais memorabilia. *Rue d'Etretat.*

Hypermarkets: Le Havre has two: **Mammouth** and **Auchan**, though the distance from the ferry terminal to Mammouth makes Auchan (in the Haute Ville, some 4 kilometres from the centre) a far better bet for the bargain-hunting British; bus number 71 leaves place des Halles for Auchan every fifteen minutes. And don't forget that however many hundreds of francs you spend, no credit cards are accepted.

There are two street **markets**, one on Monday, Wednesday and Friday along avenue René Coty just in front of the tourist office and the other on the Rond Pont spilling along cours de la République, on Tuesday, Thursday and Saturday.

A Place to Stay

Le Havre, being such a large city, has a lot of hotels of which the following are a small, personally visited, selection.

Celtic: the friendly young couple who run the Celtic, the décor and the simple rooms are all immediately welcoming and, according to the proprietors, they are used to greeting English families 'who put two or three days aside at the end of their holiday to spend in Le Havre'. A spotless spot. There is a car park but no restaurant. Unusually, you pay for your room in advance. *Rue Voltaire,* ☎ *35 42 39 77. Moderate.*

Voltaire: with its rooms all leading off a central corridor on the same floor, this hotel feels more like a private apartment and you have to be on your best whispering behaviour. M. Louage keeps an extremely proper, well-furnished establishment, thoroughly deserving of its one star. *Rue Voltaire,* ☎ *35 41 30 91. Inexpensive to moderate.*

Des Phares: up in Ste Adresse, this fine-looking white villa decorated with pink geraniums (as everyone described it when we asked for directions) is run by a lively, enthusiastic Mme Morgand who is in her high-octane seaside-landlady mode at breakfast, ferrying unlimited vacuum flasks of coffee to the long, communal table surrounded by family memorabilia. You are more likely to find yourself sharing the bread basket with French reps than fellow mini-breakers. The bedrooms, mostly in a separate, chalet-style building next door, have candlewick bedspreads and cheap, plywood furnishings but they serve their utilitarian purpose and are comfortable. *Rue Général de Gaulle,* ☎ *35 46 31 86. Inexpensive to moderate.*

Suisse: a small hotel, its fourteen rooms conveniently situated opposite the shops, theatre and cafés of espace Niemeyer. Have patience – having climbed the spiral staircase to reach Reception on the first floor, the staff do not exactly jump to attention, but it's worth staying here if only for the disarming view over Le Havre's cultural hub and the port beyond. And the prices. *Rue Racine,* ☎ *35 42 37 05. Inexpensive to moderate.*

Bordeaux: occupying a prestigious site on the espace Niemeyer this modern three-star is principally a businessman's hotel and ranks among the best in town. Its thirty-one soundproofed rooms are well equipped with private TV, mini-bar, direct-dial telephone, etc. *Rue Louis Brindeau,* ☎ *35 22 69 44. Expensive.*

And Somewhere to Eat

The town, as distinct from the region, is not famous for its cuisine, although, as in other parts of Normandy, lunchtime is sacrosanct – the Le Havre traffic wardens all pack up between 12 and 2 p.m. for lunch and you can legally park then free of charge. In celebration of their hero, Niemeyer, the only food they named after him was a chocolate in a box the shape of the cultural centre 'yogurt pot'. But this is France and though you can eat superbly well without wrecking the purse the places need a little bit more ferreting out than in other ports.

La Chaumette: 'Wow, that's one big mother of a lobster!' was how one American greeted certainly the biggest lobster we've ever seen. Chef and owner Mme Frechet specialises in fish of equal or lesser proportions. Don't be put off by the fake beams and the thatched over-cute entrance. *Rue Racine,* ☎ *35 43 66 80. Moderate to expensive.*

Lescalle: under its previous ownership this was Jean Paul Sartre's favourite dining room while he worked as a teacher from 1931 to 1933 in the town's Lycée François I. Its art nouveau décor and prime location on two corners of the square keeps it amongst the smartest in town. *Pl. de l'Hôtel de Ville,* ☎ *35 43 07 93. Moderate.*

Le Beau Séjour: don't be misled by the bright, flashing neon name – this restaurant is not the amusement arcade it looks, but one of the best eating places in town, just one huge room with a view. If you are lucky enough to get a window seat (specify when booking), the whole bay, the dusk activity of strollers, dogs and sailors and sunset-lit chalet roofs lie before you. The dining room is large, the service is top class, the tablecloths, napkins and waiters' jackets crisply white and the menus leatherbound. The fish is superb, in fact the restaurant calls itself 'La Maison du Homard et du Poisson' – even the hors d'oeuvre pastries are in the shape of a fish. *Pl. Clemenceau, Ste Adresse,* ☎ *35 46 19 69. Moderate.*

La Petite Auberge: on the road to Ste Adresse, this olde worlde building has been heavily patronised by locals ever since Michelin awarded its cuisine one of their coveted red 'R' ratings. Booking is essential. *Rue de Ste Adresse,* ☎ *31 46 27 32. Moderate.*

Brasserie Weekend: a no-nonsense eating house with marble-topped tables, a tiled floor and a bar built out of a boat which, perhaps because of its jukebox (selectors at your table), attracts a youngish crowd. *Ste Adresse. Inexpensive.*

Brasserie du Théâtre: looking more than a smart cafeteria, part-under-cover and part-open air in the shadow of the concrete yogurt pot. Dishes such as *cassoulet*, tripe in cream sauce and lamb kidney kebabs appear on a formidable menu. It is very popular with students who voted it the best in town, which it probably is, taking into account the average student's budget. A good place to sit, stare and read the (house) newspapers, and there's a popular piano bar which opens till late every night, famous for its 101 different drinks. *Espace Oscar Niemeyer*, ☎ *35 21 54 44. Inexpensive to moderate.*

Deauville Bar: one of the most popular spots for sitting and watching the Le Havre world go by. Basic snacks and light meals. *Av. René Coty, no telephone. Inexpensive.*

La Cave: not quite a restaurant but more than a café, La Cave serves crêpes, delicious cakes, ice-creams, omelettes and toasted sandwiches (*croque-monsieurs*). There is no chance of your ice-cream melting inside – the café is in a basement, as cool as a church crypt in all but a heat wave. A few outside seats are available if you don't mind the exhaust fumes on the busy Avenue René Coty. ☎ *35 21 14 78. Inexpensive.*

Le Nuage dans la Tasse: young and enthusiastic Mme Lefèbre ended her teaching career and worked voluntarily in a Parisian tea-room for a while before opening this *salon de thé* and *tarterie* last July. It is furnished in *nouvelles meubles* with a few tasteful pictures on the walls, big jugs of flowers, lace curtains and a few tables and black wooden chairs – just the place for dropping laden shopping bags and saying you can go no further. At lunchtime Mme Lefèbre prepares three or four imaginative salads (for example, rice, prunes and tuna or pineapple, carrots and cabbage) and hot vegetable tarts, but by tea-time she is on to huge cups of *café Viennoise* (coffee with naughty but nice Chantilly cream), tea and delicious cakes. *Av. Foch,* ☎ *35 21 64 94. Inexpensive.*

Cambridge: you'll find this fish restaurant hard to beat in any of the Channel ports. The specialities change daily and include turbot, John Dory and salmon from Scotland; the livelier specimens are kept in the aquarium behind the bar in the centre of the restaurant. Many of the dishes carry cream sauces, naturally since this is Normandy. The owner speaks good English – she used to work in the tourist office. There are two floors, the top more comfortable in hot weather since the windows, overlooking the cultural centre, open onto a small balcony. Pink tablecloths and beautiful china plates. *Rue Voltaire,* ☎ *35 43 50 24. Moderate to expensive.*

Nuts and Bolts

Townsend Thoresen sail from Portsmouth, and Irish Continental Line ferries have services from Rosslare and Cork. For on-going travellers Le Havre forms the pivot of a huge communications network linking England with Germany, Switzerland and Belgium as well as France, hence its long popularity with passing-through visitors. The autoroute can be picked up just 2 kilometres from the city centre, and Paris is only two hours (200 kilometres) away.

You might imagine from Le Havre's size that the passenger port was a long way away from the centre, but it isn't. Bus number 2 runs from the Rond Pont, stopping at Hôtel de Ville, or it is an easy twenty-minute walk.

The tourist office is located next to the town hall in place de l'Hôtel de Ville, near the junction of rue Général Leclerc and avenue René Coty. Like most tourist offices, it operates a hotel booking service. In 1987 it is due to move round the back of the current building and may have moved already (☎ 35 21 22 88).

There is ample parking in the town centre, often free for the first hour.

Around and About

The Seine-Maritime (originally, though not disparagingly, known as la Seine Inférieure) is not unlike the Weald of Kent. Lying to the north of the swift-flowing Seine it is fairly flat, even marshy in parts, chequered with small fields and the occasional river, and backed by the chalk country, the Pays de Caux, whose open farmlands reach out to Rouen. But despite these similarities with Kent, the Seine-Maritime has an unmistakably Norman stamp. There are scores of tiny hamlets made up of thatched wooden cottages, pastures of creamy cattle (Normandy's six million cattle produce a quarter of the country's demand for dairy produce) and apple and cherry orchards. Up the coastline from Le Havre is the milky Côte d'Albâtre, the Alabaster Coast, 120 kilometres of impressive chalk cliffs, particularly attractive to birdwatchers and walkers and best seen at Etretat with its famous arches and needle (see Dieppe, p. 87). There are more than thirty lively resorts and quieter beaches, each one nestled in its own valley that leads down to the sea.

Inland, the paucity of hills makes the Seine-Maritime an ideal region for walkers and cyclists. In the nose of countryside between Le Havre and Fécamp, for example, there are miles of well-signposted footpaths suitable for a few hours' or a few days' hiking and a whole network of meandering lanes for the two-wheel traveller. And if you happen to be here in the cherry season you'll find refreshment provided at stalls all along the roadsides.

The region of fishing ports like Honfleur, and the grand resorts like Cabourg, Deauville, Houlgate and Trouville to the south-west of Le Havre, across the Seine estuary, flourished in the period of 'La Belle Epoque'. Elegant, luxurious hotels, exciting casinos, Thalasso-therapeutic spas, tennis courts, racecourses, sailing clubs, and, of course, bathing huts and machines, were all built to attract and amuse the rich, the titled, and even the royal visitors who flocked from Paris and from across the Channel. Today many of the hotels have been bought by modern groups and reconditioned to meet our less imaginative, more sanitised tastes, and new apartment blocks have been built overlooking the golden sandy beaches for summer renters and retirers. The water along this stretch of coastline is perfect for swimming, as centuries of cliff erosion has left an underwater shelf stretching two kilometres out to sea.

Honfleur

You can just about see Honfleur across the estuary of the Seine, but the only way to approach by car is to head inland, cross the river at the Tancarville suspension bridge and drive back west along the other bank, following a route across the broad, flat flood plain of the towering poplar-lined Seine.

Unless the sight of oil refineries and other industrial monuments excites you, you'll find the actual suburbs of Le Havre, which stretch along the banks of the Seine, extremely uninspiring.

However, since the opening in 1959 of the Tancarville bridge, which suddenly appears round a corner like the Golden Gate, 26 kilometres (16 miles) to the east of Le Havre, the town has a vital direct link to the south. The A15 dual-carriageway leads from Le Havre, behind smoky factories and, a few minutes later, past the sheer, white cliffs of the gorge to the bridge and on to the A13 Caen–Paris autoroute.

Honfleur's Amsterdam-in-miniature appearance clearly reveals its maritime history which has been well documented since the fourteenth century. As a fortified town it played an important part in the Hundred Years' War and was, in fact, occupied by the English from 1419 to 1450. In the sixteenth and seventeenth centuries Honfleur was a busy fishing and commercial port and the birth-place of numerous navigators (Samuel Champlain made the first of many Canadian voyages from here and discovered Quebec in 1608). But with the gradual silting up of the Seine the town's importance dwindled, especially as neighbouring Le Havre grew in stature; it is still a thriving fishing port, threaded with nets to trip the unwary, and echoing to the screams of scavenging seagulls, but the historic basin now carries the sounds of halyards rattling against the masts of yachts.

Narrow, tile-faced, historic houses – some seven storeys tall, and many with cafés, restaurants, antique stores and galleries on the quayside – sit tightly packed around three sides of the Vieux Bassin. They are the subject of many an artist's canvas, especially the last in the row, the twin-turreted remains of Honfleur's sixteenth-century Governor's house. The fourth side forms part of the main coast road except when it rises Tower-Bridge style to let yachts pass out to sea. Behind the Vieux Bassin lie the steeply sloping cobbled streets and alleyways around the church of Ste-Catherine. This fifteenth-century church was built entirely of wood (apart from the foundations) by the port's shipwrights, the nave actually construc-ted with ships' hulls in the shape of a keel. It is illuminated nightly, as is the nearby weatherboarded belfry. The best streets for admir-ing the old houses of Honfleur are rue Haute, rue de l'Homme de Bois, rue de Puits, rue Brulée, rue de la Bavole, rue de la Prison and rue de la Ville.

Apart from admiring Honfleur's good looks, it is an ideal place for a fish lunch, the catch on the menu being landed, in some cases, no more than twenty yards from the pavement tables. As well as the restaurants surrounding the Vieux Bassin there are others along quai de la Quarantaine with acres of outside seating: L'Ecluse, L'Absinthe (expensive), Bistro du Port (grills on an open fire), Brasserie au Bon Cidre (least expensive) and Les Deux Ponts (mainly à la carte). For its size, Honfleur has more than a fair share of interesting shops; one worth a special mention is Neptune on rue Montpensier which sells ships in bottles, Breton sweaters, matelot shirts, genuine Docksides and other real outdoor McCoys for sailors.

With all these pluses, Honfleur draws the summer crowds – but who can blame them for here is a port that ought to be airlifted lock, stock and bollard and dropped into Earl's Court for the Boat Show. Above all, it is genuine, right down to the ancient chemist sign painted on a slate wall recommending 'cures for seasickness'.

Hôtel du Dauphin: half-timbered on the ground floor and typical slate-fronted upper three storeys. Two-star and efficiently run. *Pl. Pierre Berthelot,* ☎ *31 89 15 53. Inexpensive to moderate.*

Hostellerie Lechat: stone-built and ivy covered, this three-star hotel looks superbly manorial, situated next to Ste-Catherine's wooden church in the heart of the old, old town (as distinct from the ancient remainder of Honfleur). Full of beams, wood panelling and rustic furniture, the hotel has an excellent restaurant decorated with a live-seafood tank. If you prefer, and don't mind a bit of street noise, there is outside seating in the square. *Pl. Ste-Catherine,* ☎ *31 89 23 85. Moderate to expensive.*

Restaurant L'Eau Vive: if it's lunchtime and you haven't yet reached Honfleur, stop at this delightful, hidden-away restaurant at Fatouville-Grestain just where route N180 meets the N312 from the Tancarville bridge. Turn off the road, park in the car park and climb the stone steps up to the cosy half-timbered building sitting in attractive gardens (there's even a small lake and a caravan site tucked away in the grounds). *Fatouville-Grestain,* ☎ *32 57 67 44. Moderate.*

Deauville

Deauville reeks of conspicuous consumption. The town, 'created' by the Duke of Morny in the 1860s on the Côte Fleurie, has long been esteemed by the rich and famous and it is still unrivalled as the classiest, most upmarket beach resort in northern France. The sandy beach, lapped by calm, shallow blue water, is half covered by a sea of red, blue and yellow windbreaks and rows of what look like Henry V's Agincourt tents. It is a curious sight for the British, who are familiar with angling their deck chairs to face both sea and sun, to see the Deauville crowds lined up facing the 'wrong' way. But at least they get to keep an eye on the passing parade; starlet-spotting is best practised on the Planches, a boardwalk promenade that runs the length of the beach and still as chic and fashionable as it was in the days when Europe's royalty and nobility patronised the town. And still do – both the Queen and Prince Charles have paid recent visits. To the east of the Planches, you'll find the Port Deauville marina which holds some 900 yachts and extends from the mouth of the river Touques to the harbour entrance, providing many a weary yachtsman with an alluring break from the rigours of life on the high seas.

The town is also a firm favourite with rich Americans, Elizabeth Taylor among them (who stays at the Normandy), and there are branches of all the elegant names in shopping to cater for such wealthy custom, including Hermès, Ted Lapidus and Yves St Laurent, all housed in what look more like 'cottages'; even Printemps has excelled itself with an upmarket brown-and-white façade, a respite from the familiar green flowery logo. It all makes the familiar prospect of hypermarket shopping several bank accounts removed.

Deauville has two casinos, one for the crowds in summer, opening from March 15 to September 15, and a second for the remaining six months of the year, when a large proportion of Deauville is in hibernation. There is also a modern thalassotherapy centre, a white, art deco, Olympic-size swimming pool, a golf course, four riding schools, twenty tennis courts, several nightclubs and courses for horses that attract jockeys from all over the world – at La Touques (flat) and Clairefontaine (flat and steeplechasing).

Hôtel Normandy: at practically every point in Deauville you can see the Normandy. The approach to the main entrance, with its perfectly trimmed hedges, fleets of French-plated Rollers, manicured lawns and flowerbeds, is indicative of its baronial aspirations. The opulence of the interior resembles the Ritz. The Normandy is huge, spread out in long rows of heavy-eaved buildings, with 310 sumptuous rooms and fittingly giant-sized public rooms decorated with chandeliers, potted palms, marble columns, stucco ceilings and the posh works. Top of the price bracket but nothing in Deauville comes cheap. And just Deauville does for the address. (☎ *31 88 09 21.) Expensive.*

Trouville

The French novelist Flaubert once complained that 'the beach where I once ran around naked is now adorned with policemen and there are demarcation lines for the two sexes'. He was writing during the early nineteenth century when Trouville became a fashionable retreat with its own salon and bathing cabins for ladies to take to the waters in privacy. How things have changed. Today Trouville is predominantly a family holiday resort with wide sands and safe bathing, as well as an active fishing port. With just one casino, a less glittery beach boardwalk than at Deauville, a few less tennis courts and a lot more children, you could call it a poor man's Deauville.

Manoir du Grand Bec: this hotel/restaurant is actually situated halfway between Honfleur and Trouville; a tall, detached, half-timbered mansion set on the clifftop just off the road but impossible to miss. The Manoir is worth a stay or just a pause to sample their delicious fish on the terrace overlooking the sea. Both hotel and restaurant prices are a little higher than average – but then so is the quality. *Villerville,* ☎ *31 88 09 88. Moderate restaurant, expensive rooms.*

Rouen

It would be sacrilege to visit Normandy without visiting Rouen. One of Europe's most historic towns, the ancient capital of the region sits astride the Seine with scores of meticulously restored, half-timbered fourteenth- to seventeenth-century houses all twisted and gnarled by the years. The Cathedral of Notre Dame, one of the very finest in France, rises majestically from the end of rue du Gros Horloge in a blend of architectural styles, eleventh-century influences merging with twelfth, sixteenth and seventeenth. Its two towers are quite incongruous, the older twelfth-century Gothic St Romain on the left, the more opulent seventeenth-century Butter Tower on the right (so called because of contributions paid to the church by those caught eating butter during the Lent fasting period).

Rouen enjoys the dubious honour of being the place where Joan of Arc was burnt at the stake by the English in 1431. The site, place du Vieux Marché, is now marked by a new church that looks like a giant crocodile. The Joan of Arc Museum stands in place du Vieux Marché with a collection of relics telling of her unfortunate imprisonment, trial and eventual execution.

Rouen is also famous for its Gros Horloge, a spectacular clock with a blue, gold and red face mounted on an archway above the road of the same name, and a collection of world-famous Impressionist paintings in the Musée des Beaux Arts. Buy a ticket to see the intricate inner workings of the Gros Horloge and the same ticket will admit you to the Musée des Beaux Arts and the Musée de Ferronnerie, a bizarre collection of doorknockers, jewellery, kitchen utensils and others, all made of iron.

Place Jeanne d'Arc, originally the market square, and place de la Cathédrale are lined with jostling cafés, the places to head for an *espresso* before window shopping and famous-building spotting.

Hôtel de la Cathédrale: hugging a central, flower-filled courtyard in the heart of the town's pedestrian area is the slightly olde worlde Hôtel de la Cathédrale. It has twenty or so rooms, individually decorated though all fairly basic. It is nevertheless very popular, so book well in advance. *Rue St Romain,* ☎ *35 71 57 95. Moderate.*

Le Vieux Marché: the dining room in this brasserie-cum-restaurant is huge, and spills out onto the pavement. It has a rambling menu, so keep your order simple – this is not the place to go for gastronomic treats but it is a lively place, especially because of its location, and it is open till very late. *Pl. du Vieux Marché,* ☎ *35 75 59 09. Inexpensive.*

La Boucherie: on the way to Rouen in a tiny village called Les

Vertus, this pretty, Norman-style restaurant would serve you well after a morning spent behind a laden trolley in nearby Mammouth. Its high-quality meals are so popular that the restaurant has ceased to advertise, so don't forget to book in advance. *Les Vertus*, ☎ *35 84 83 10. Moderate.*

Route des Abbayes

Follow the D182 road from Le Havre to Rouen. It hugs the meanders of the Seine but you must be patient because it takes a while before you finally shake off the grim and smelly landscape of oil refineries and general industrialisation of outskirts Le Havre. The very word Seine comes from the Celtic word *squan*, meaning to curve, and curve it does, gently falling at the rate of just one foot for every mile of meander. By the time you reach the rather curious white cliffs at Tancarville with its massive suspension bridge – Normandy's answer to the Firth of Forth – the scenery has become lovely and rural, particularly when you pass through the Brotonne Forest and regional nature reserve.

This route, along the river Seine, is known as the 'Road of the Abbeys' linking the Romanesque church of St Martin de Boscherville to the awesome ruins of the Benedictine abbey at Jumièges, one of the greatest ruins in the whole of France. At Caudebec-en-Caux, situated on a broad elbow of the Seine, you'll find the flamboyantly Gothic 'Church of Our Lady', in other words another Notre Dame, built between 1425 and 1539 and described by Henry IV as 'the most beautiful chapel in my kingdom'. At St Wandrille there are the remains of the town's Benedictine abbey transept. On the southern bank of the river is the Brotonne, the largest forest in the Seine-Maritime and a national conservation area. Your route will also take you through the small towns of La Bouille, Duclair, Caudebec-en-Caux (where Victor Hugo's daughter was drowned – before its silting up the river used to be extremely rough just here) and Villequier where you can visit the Maison Vacquerie, a museum devoted to Victor Hugo memorabilia, as well as sample local cuisine and find places to stay. The road also passes under both the Tancarville and Brotonne suspension bridges.

Roscoff

A town more maligned by those who have never been yet more loved by those who have would be difficult to find. But the reason for Roscoff's unjustifiably meagre reputation among outsiders is obvious. As far as most of its British visitors are concerned, Roscoff is merely a place where the boat stops to let off their cars on the first leg of their journey to wherever.

Most people arriving in Roscoff do so at the new deep-water, all-states-of-the-tide jetty created in 1970, some 1½ kilometres (a twenty-minute walk) east of the town. Despite the alluring prose in the town's brochure urging visitors to 'come to Roscoff without hesitation, an agreeable stay is guaranteed', most just edge down the ferry ramp and, to their enormous loss, head straight off for all points south. Even more surprising is the fact that Roscoff's thousands of day-trippers also give the town a miss, preferring to catch the bus to Morlaix's Euromarché, some 20 kilometres away, instead of shopping on their doorstep.

According to the tourist office, those who do decide to linger for a day before continuing with their travel often alter their plans to include two or three days in Roscoff at the very end of their holiday. You could well spend a week here without having to make any excuses, and, as the French say, profit from the experience. But while most visitors to the port remain blissfully ignorant of the Roscoff pleasures, it makes it all the more interesting for those who do give it a try.

The town is the smallest of all the Channel ports; as a measure of its scale you'll find that lots of hotels, restaurants and shops don't even print a street address on their business cards, let alone a number. Small but beautiful is the description that instinctively flits to mind.

Roscoff's grey granite or bleached white, slate-roof buildings and sharply trimmed gardens are only half the pretty picture. The shoreline, broken by jetties and a few sandy beaches, looks out upon a remarkable scene of sky and a sea pierced in a hundred places by ragged teeth of granite that have torn the hulls of many a wayward vessel. The French historian Michelet wrote: 'The sea is English by nature – she doesn't like France. She breaks our ships. The whole coast is a cemetery.' Largest of the rocks is the Ile de Batz, a must to visit no matter how short your stay.

One visiting German tour operator once threatened to sue the tourist board, claiming their brochure pictures, which showed lavish expanses of beach, were fraudulent. They suggested he came back six hours later which he did, and apologised. As the massive tide creeps out, 5 metres in all from top to bottom, leaving the port's crab-fishing boats balanced on crutches (to keep them upright as they sit on the sea bed) Roscoff effectively doubles in size.

Roscoff's population of 4000 also more than doubles with its, mostly French, summer visitors – who themselves probably feel rather foreign in this Breton-speaking half of Brittany. But Roscoff has not sold out to the obvious traits of holiday commercialism. The town's controlled development is best reflected in a pizzeria we spotted, housed in a modest olde worlde cottage building with white shutters. With just the tiniest, highly discreet neon sign it seemed a far cry from Pizza Hut.

Roscoff's history is rather less refined. French accounts of the town's yesteryears refer frequently to *pillage et massacre* by the Normans, the Romans and the English. We really shouldn't be welcomed here at all. In 1374 the English burnt the Russian-sounding Rosko Goz, the ancient site of the present town, to the ground. But the Scots should feel more at home since it was to these shores that Mary Stuart came in 1548 when she was just six years old to be presented to the court of the King of France. Ten years later she was married to the country's dauphin. The house in which she supposedly stayed still stands, as do its Tudor windows;

and La Tour Stuart, part of the town's ancient foundations, still bears her name as do one or two Mary Stuart this and Mary Stuart that establishments that have turned such links to commercial advantage for the benefit of British visitors. Bonnie Prince Charlie also came here after his defeat at Culloden although, judging from the lack of Bonnie anything here, he obviously didn't make the same impression.

Roscoff peaked in commercial importance in the fourteenth and fifteenth centuries. It was the site of a massive market where traders from the Hanseatic ports used to meet those from the Mediterranean to exchange goods, often overwintering in the same nearby sheltered anchorages that are today so popular with British yachtsmen. Grand granite mansions belonging to the wealthy Roscovite ship-owners can still be admired today. But Roscoff's most famous commerce is perhaps its Johnnies who came over here on their bicycles carrying onions from the Golden Belt of arable lands around St Pol de Léon. And did *you* know that the first Johnny to embark for England was Henri Olivier in 1828? . . . Well most Roscovite children do.

Do Not Miss

The quayside of the **Vieille Porte**, built in 1623, and the narrow concrete 600-metre jetty that leaps out to sea and serves as the low-tide boat-landing spot for the ferries to the Ile de Batz, is the most popular spot in town for a stroll. The rows of bright blue crab pots, fishing boats, nets and old Roscovite salts are easy game for anyone armed with a camera. The cafés and bars surrounding the old port, such as Ty Pier and Chez Janie, are the popular places for the evening gather, fuelled by pastis and fugged by plumes of Gauloises.

Roscoff is an important centre for studying marine biology. The Centre of Oceanographic Research, affiliated to the Sorbonne in Paris, is the most important in Europe – they even named the pretty main square of the town place Lacaze-Duthiers, after the Sorbonne zoologist who established the Centre in 1872. The attached **Aquarium Charles Perez** and **Musée Océanographique**, whose displays include Channel specimens (day-trippers included), is open every day from Easter to September (in winter for pre-arranged groups only). *Place Georges Teissier.*

A 350-year-old fig tree, **Le Grand Figuier**, stands close to the town centre in the garden of an old Capuchin convent. Old it may be, and heavily supported by granite crutches, but some years it still manages to produce over 800 pounds of fruit.

You can always get your bearings from Roscoff's sixteenth-century church, **l'Eglise Notre Dame de Croas-Batz**, in place Lacaze-Duthiers. Its distinctive Renaissance three-tiered belfry is one of the most ornate in Finistère. Classical concerts, as well as more modern music, are played here throughout the summer.

Walk from here along boulevard Carnot and you'll pass a cluster of tiny white-sanded beaches, seven in all and highly popular with swimmers, dinghy sailors and windsurfers, while less active generations, many of whom are here to benefit from the iodised air and to take treatments at the two **thalassotherapy centres**, watch the goings on from the promenade gardens filled with palms, stubby tamarisk bushes and old-fashioned street lamps. There's also a sheltered children's beach with swings that carry their horror-struck passengers out across the shallows.

Roscoff's weather is gentle, created by a rather temperate series of micro-climates. Its sea airs, which may come from any quarter, have long attracted convalescents and, since the foundation of Europe's first thalassotherapy centre in 1899, those suffering from rheumatism and arthritis. Apart from the French, the cures are most popular with Germans, who find the algae treatments, massages and pools more beneficial than the ailing British (l'Institut de Roch-Kroum seems to attract more of the British quota than the alternative centre, La Clinique Kerlena). A week's treatment at the Thalassotherapy Centre, comprising six supervised sessions, costs around £150 excluding accommodation. The season peaks in spring and autumn. For details write to BP 28 29211 Roscoff (☎ 98 69 72 15).

Shopping Spree

Roscoff is not an exciting place to visit if you rank shopping high on your list of Channel port priorities. Apart from a rash of tedious souvenir-gift shops (though nowhere near as many as its 'counterports' to the east), there's nothing wrong with its shops – it's just that there aren't really enough of them to last a visit.

Le Cormoran: a small outlet selling woollen sweaters for men, women and children direct from the factory. *Rue Albert du Mur.*

Les Mouettes: 'We only speak a little English but we are real friendly' reads the notice on the window of this mini gift-shop opposite the church. Beachware, Indian fabrics, a few toys and various cute ornaments as well as a range of kitchenware are its stock in trade. *Rue Albert du Mur.*

Les Récifs: fall in love with Roscoff's seascapes and here's where you'll find them on canvas. This small gallery seems to specialise in oil paintings, with one-man exhibitions usually devoted to the works of local artists. *Rue Albert du Mur.*

RoscoGoz: taking its name from the town's ancient core, here is an Aladdin's cave of Breton sweaters, matelot striped shirts, white duffel coats, wet-weather sailors' gear along with souvenirs like Breton dolls, hand-painted pipes and postcards. *Rue Amiral Réveillère.*

Guyadez: opposite RoscoGoz sits this attractive pâtisserie and *salon de thé* with a window display devoted to sweets shaped as sardines, seagull eggs, scallops, and other seaside disguises. They sell Galettes Roscovites, and a Breton speciality, Galichons: a caramel made from salted butter and sold in fancy boxes and ceramic pots. *Rue Amiral Réveillère.*

Maison de la Presse: on the corner with Armand Rousseau, this is the place where you can buy maps, cigarettes and English newspapers hot off the last ferry. *Rue Amiral Réveillère.*

Monique Léon Potteries: open only during the summer, locally born Mme Léon's superb pottery is all hand- and home-made. *Rue Amiral Réveillère.*

Pâtisserie Marie Stuart: heavy italic script presses home the historic allegiances of this tea-room. Mock street lamps, marble-topped tables and bentwood chairs complete a slightly over-the-top ambience, but the opening hours – from 7 a.m. till 11 p.m. –

and the ice-creams of knickerbocker proportions plus Breton gâteaux made from real butter, make it all seem rather wonderful. *Rue Amiral Réveillère.*

Gallerie Morgane: mini Madame Morgane seems lost in her crypt-like gallery where Mary Stuart supposedly slept before embarking in 1548 (a plaque on the outside wall confirms the building's pedigree). She (mini Madame) sells an odd collection of mostly local paintings and wood carvings. *Rue Amiral Réveillère.*

Boucherie du Port: M et Mme Jegoudez' large delicatessen, tucked down a side-street, is a haven for *fromages à la coupe*, wines, pâtés, saucissons, big jars of *choucroute* and *cassoulet* and wax-sealed jars of Pommery mustard. Effectively a two-in-one shop, they also sell piping hot pieces of quiche ready to take away and rôtisserie-cooked poultry. Open seven days a week, until at least 7 p.m. *Rue Gambetta.*

Claude Hamon: stoop low as you enter the door of this converted fisherman's house which now houses displays of furniture and maritime bygones collected by Claude Hamon. Open daily during the summer. *Rue Gambetta.*

The **Euromarché** at nearby Morlaix plays a key role in the standard day-trippers' itinerary. After an overnight crossing to Roscoff, passengers jump on the waiting bus to the hypermarket, followed by a lunch and a browse round Morlaix's historic centre (see p. 154), returning to catch the ferry home.

Roscoff is too small to support an open-air market, but the nearest is just a ten-minute drive away in St Pol de Léon on Thursday mornings.

A Place to Stay

Thalassotherapy dictates a lengthy hotel season, beginning in March and lasting till mid-November, though many close in winter (as do a large number of the shops and restaurants). Both thalas-sotherapy centres are open all year round and account mainly for the tripling of Roscoff's population in July and August. Some of the hotels, in fact, advertise their locations not only in terms of distance from the sea but also from the Institute of Thalassotherapy: '*Face à la mer et près des cures*'.

Gulf Stream: Roscoff's three-star Ritz, a big detached building surrounded by its own lawn and flowerbedded gardens, and a short walk from the town centre. Jacques Creach's acclaimed restaurant overlooks a quiet expanse of beach. His nouvelle cuisine dishes are served with great style – a trio of bow-tied waiters co-ordinate their raising of three guests' terrines (parties of six or more might experience two-handed compromises). Don't miss the Carmen Miranda-coloured sorbet dessert. *Rosko Goz*, ☎ *98 69 73 19. Moderate to expensive.*

Les Tamaris: last summer a young couple, ex-owners of a series of Ibis hotels, bought and carried out a superb Habitat-esque conversion of the former Hôtel des Saisons de Tamaris, extending it from five to twenty-three rooms. Impressions of spaciousness, lightness airiness, newness and spotlessness pervade, thanks not least to an abundance of pale beech furniture and floorboards. The hotel could be anywhere but one look out of the windows overlooking the ocean and Ile de Batz will give you unambiguous bearings. *Rue Edouard-Corbière*, ☎ *98 61 22 99. Moderate.*

La Résidence: a new extension built onto the end wall has changed the mural name to Ho La but it is otherwise the same modern solidly furnished and respectable place. What it sadly lacks in charm it makes up for in calmness, thanks to its location in a quiet residential street. All the thirty-two rooms are well furnished and most have balconies overlooking gardens, though none overlook the sea. *Rue des Johnnies*, ☎ *98 69 74 85. Moderate.*

D'Angleterre: a superbly grand building, dominated by two slate capped towers, draped with ivy, decorated by geraniums and flavoured by white louvred shutters. The interior, with its cane furniture and crocheted cushion covers, conservatory lounge white-beamed restaurant, and a gorgeous, well-tended and secluded garden had the feel more of colonial hill country than a cross-Channel port. When we checked in the reception was manned by Mme Quément's new baby, the kitchen by her brother (the chef), so, despite the manorial appearances, the family-at home mood pervades. *Rue Albert du Mun,* ☎ *98 69 70 42. Moderate.*

Des Bains: one of the town's historic hostelries – the nearest equivalent to an old English coaching inn – originally established exclusively to accommodate those who came to medically imbibe the airs and waters. The hotel has a rather austere entrance hall – a stone church-like porch lined with chunky, dark, carved Breton furniture. Walk in with your cases and you are almost in a position to dive headlong into the beautiful briny slapping against the rocks. The restaurant's floor-to-ceiling glass window takes good advantage of the sea's proximity, as does the menu – in English and featuring lots of fish. Thirty-one of its fifty rooms, some like cottages, with French windows leading onto a very private sun-trap garden overlooking the sea, are in a converted stable annexe a few doors along the street. Five floors but there's a lift with naughty French postcards to help pass the time. *Rue Amiral Réveillère,* ☎ *98 61 20 65. Moderate.*

Talabardon: next door to Des Bains, opposite the churchyard and sharing similar views from its restaurant, the Talabardon was founded as the Grand in 1916. As you can verify from an interesting scrapbook in the lobby, it then advertised full board for 5 to 6 francs a day. But here the similarities stop. Prices have risen and the Talabardon has been modernised, for better for some people, for worse for others. There is, for example, a front sun-lounge and an extension on the back providing several rooms with sliding windows and balconies looking onto the sea. Polished, fairly formal in a businessy way with forty-one rooms. The restaurant, surprisingly for its location, features a good deal of meat along with variations on the fish-theme. Also soup with profiteroles though we did not chance it. *Pl. de l'Eglise,* ☎ *98 61 24 95. Moderate.*

Des Arcades: a bar with rooms; the former is the popular, noisy gathering spot for the restless local youth who spill over into the lounge area and the pavement beneath the sixteenth-century granite arches (the arcades in the name of the hotel). The second and third floors look for reasons unknown like a Swiss chalet. If you can tolerate the action below, the simple rooms and grand sea views will more than compensate. *Rue Amiral Réveillère,* ☎ *98 69 70 45. Inexpensive to moderate.*

And Somewhere to Eat

You are probably best advised to dine in your hotel since the restaurants are, with the exception of crêperies, thin on the ground. But there are these:

La Brocherie: *'manger à la Brocherie, c'est prolonger la vie'*, maintains manic Georges Fabre, the chef, owner and the self-confessed unofficial ambassador of England on account of the number of natives who patronise his establishment. And who can blame them when a set meal starts at less than £6 and the à la carte includes lobsters and, his speciality, brochettes of either fish or chicken, all served in the second oldest house in Roscoff. *Rue Edouard-Corbière, near the Aquarium,* ☎ *98 61 20 98. Inexpensive to moderate.*

Le Homard: tucked behind an elbow of road and easily missed on your way into town, this tiny, newly opened, family-run ex-pizzeria feels like being in someone's dining room. Simple but cheerful décor with clever use of space – they haven't made a mistake of cramming people in like the sardines they serve. Other dishes, which do include *homards* (one brand of lobster, the other being *langouste*), are served through a hatch, while hors d'oeuvres are neatly laid out on a buffet table. *Rue Albert de Mur. Moderate.*

Café de la Poste: this busy, low-beamed and smoky-atmosphere crêperie is the best in town, selling savoury-filled galettes and sweet crêpes at low prices, plus fish soup, mussels and a few other non-pancake items. *Rue Gambetta. Inexpensive.*

Auberge du Quai: lively open-plan café-bar in one half, and a restaurant decorated with stuffed birds, dried flowers, carved Breton furniture and raw brick walls in the other. No special meals, just honest, decent and truthful omelettes, steaks and salads. Hard on the busy jetty with plenty of ringside seats for watching the passing procession. *Quai Parmentier. Inexpensive to moderate.*

Nuts and Bolts

It was not until 1972 that the first ferry service started from England (and 1978 from Ireland). Brittany Ferries now operate a daily six-hour service from Plymouth and occasional (weekend) nineteen-hour services to Cork (☎ 98 69 07 20). There are train services between Roscoff and Paris, direct during the summer, via Morlaix in the winter.

The well-stocked Office de Tourisme is in a building resembling a beach hut in place J-P Lejeune, BP 40/29211 Roscoff, ☎ 98 69 70 70.

Parking is never easy, especially on a summer weekend. Best place for space is on the old quay, or place Lacaze-Duthiers, both free.

Around and About

Roscoff is the most westerly Channel port and the key point of access to Finistère, the end of the world to the ancient Celts (from the Latin *finis terrae*) and the most Breton part of Brittany where some still speak the old language and wear unique costumes, and everyone enters into the spirit of the *pardons*, traditional religious Breton processions.

Although this book only covers places of interest in the immediate vicinity of Roscoff, motorists may prefer to venture much further afield and explore the spectacular scenic highlights that put Brittany second only to the Côte d'Azur in popularity for British visitors to France. The pink granite coast around Perros-Guirec, Trébeurden and Lannion, so named because of the rosy hue of its dramatic rocks, lies to the east; the sharp nose of the Crozon Peninsula, Brest and fishing ports like Audierne and Douarnenez are along the western coastline. Head south, through fields of artichokes and spring vegetables which earn the region its nickname 'France's market garden', and you'll meet the pines and beech woods of the Argoat (the 'country of woods' as distinct from the Armorica, the 'country facing the sea'), and the magically mysterious area around Heulgoat, its landscape of unusual rock formations, rivers and streams shrouded in Arthurian folklore. The rolling hills of lower Brittany ultimately lead down to coves, rivers and beaches bordered by a string of towns along the crowded southern coastline, with names like Quiberon, Morbihan and Concarneau which now roll so readily off the British tongue.

Village hopping represents an almost limitless potential – 'kant bro, kant giz, kant parrez, kant iliz', according to the words of a Breton poem ('a hundred countries, a hundred guises, a hundred parishes and a hundred churches').

Morlaix

Morlaix lies some 28 kilometres south-east of Roscoff at the end of a winding scenic road that first rides a plateau of mostly artichokes and excellent views of the sea beyond the fields and then hugs the dramatic estuary of the Bay of Morlaix. You approach the town of Morlaix along the banks of the river Dossen, its waters often congested with tied rows of yachts. Morlaix's harbour was, in fact, one of the most important in Brittany between the fifteenth and eighteenth centuries, when it served as the base for France's supreme corsair fleet whose piratic victories brought great prosperity to the town. As you enter Morlaix, you pass under the town's most striking landmark – the towering heights of a viaduct built in the 1860s to carry the Paris–Brest railway over the river gorge (pity the locals who have a demanding climb to their nearest station).

Morlaix has met the English on a memorable previous occasion. In 1522 a local corsair raided Bristol and the English replied by sending a fleet of eighty ships to ransack Morlaix. Unfortunately the English sailors got drunk, fell asleep and were massacred by the locals – hence the town's emblem which shows a French lion facing an English leopard with the motto 'If they bite you, bite them.'

Although Morlaix stands relatively far away from the ferry port, it is, surprisingly, better known to Britons disembarking at Roscoff than Roscoff itself. The main reason for this lies not so much in its historic charms, which include half-timbered houses built by wealthy merchants in the fifteenth and sixteenth centuries, but the fact that the Euromarché hypermarket stands on its outskirts and draws the Brittany Ferries excursion traffic like bees to a honeypot.

Describing itself as 'one of a new breed of shops' Morlaix's star attraction, one of the largest of France's Euromarché chain, is situated at St-Martin-des-Champs, three minutes from the centre of town on the way to Roscoff, and is open daily from 9 a.m. to 10 p.m. for the sale of food, wine, beer, records, tapes, kitchenware and household goods, clothes, gardening tools and furniture.

Hôtel d'Europe: a large and essentially a business person's hotel that dominates an island of buildings in the centre of town in the shadow of the viaduct. Reception is friendly, efficient and fluent in English, but despite antique furnishings and an impressive carved-wood staircase, the place is rather staid, quiet and lacking in personality. The fifty-eight rooms leading off sombre corridors are comfortable but uncharacteristic with remarkably thin walls. Downstairs is a slightly livelier bistro decorated in mock art nouveau style, and, what must be by far the town's finest gastronomic asset, a superb, smart but relaxed restaurant with a four-course menu which more often than not includes shrimps and prawns freshly netted in the bay. *Rue d'Aiguillon,* ☎ *98 62 11 99. Moderate.*

Ile de Batz

One of Roscoff's most exciting excursions is clearly visible from the town, lying just 1½ kilometres off the coast. The four-by-one-kilometre Ile de Batz (pronounced 'Ba'), populated by a meagre 745 inhabitants, is a timeless, unhurried community engaged in fishing, market gardening and the harvesting of seaweed for the cosmetic industry (fishermen's wives working their way along the clumps on the beaches are a familiar sight here). Tiny open ferry boats leave Roscoff's old port (at the end of the concrete jetty at low tide) at roughly hourly intervals, pick their way through the shallows with lanky weeds scraping the hull, and after a fifteen-minute crossing deposit passengers at the seaward end of the island's main lane. This leafy artery, lined in summer with wild roses, mimosa and oleander, leads to the main beach facing Roscoff, the island's three hotels and the occasional bar and shop. The modest scale of the island hardly merits a public transport system, but if walking it from end to end seems too mammoth a task, there are bicycles available for hire down by the jetty. A score of tiny sandy coves, a gentle climate, and a position far removed from noise and pollution make this a wonderful retreat, suitable, as the French say, for 'tired organisms'. St Pol de Léon retired here in 566 and lived for another thirty years to the ripe old age of 104, so it obviously has something special!

Grand Hôtel: probably the most modest grand hotel in the world, its atmosphere is more akin to a busy guesthouse in Eastbourne than Claridges. Prettily pink-rendered on the outside with a large patio where you can sit and do as little as possible except watch the tide, sailors repairing their boats and children playing on the sands. The Grand stands right beside the beach, so many of its twenty-five bedrooms have a sea view. The restaurant menus consist of imaginative variations on the fish theme as well as meaty alternatives such as calves' liver. Both rooms and meals offer outstanding value. ☎ *98 61 78 06. Inexpensive.*

Ker Nöel: an even more modest establishment from the outside but one which boasts a *chef cuisinière* called Gérard Menard who specialises in, surprise surprise, *poisson.* The nine hotel bedrooms lead from a winding wooden staircase, the fortunate ones overlooking a little front garden filled with lilies. Again a bargain place to stay. ☎ *98 61 79 98. Inexpensive.*

Château du Taureau

If you thrive on boat trips don't miss the *vedettes blanches* which leave Roscoff (again from the old port) every day from the beginning of June to the end of September at 2.30 p.m., bound for the Château du Taureau in the Baie de Morlaix. The château is a fortress built by Morlaix's townsfolk in 1542 for surveying the movements of boats on the river, following the pillaging of the town by the English.

St Pol de Léon

A small, humble market town, but home to one of Brittany's nine cathedrals and a glorious, fifteenth-century, 75-metre tower atop the Kreisker chapel which dominates the skyline for miles around like some Gothic space shuttle about to take off from its launching pad of artichokes. The town derives its name from St Paul Aurelian, a sixth-century Welsh monk who became the town's first bishop. The limestone cathedral, built between the thirteenth and sixteenth centuries, houses an interesting wooden statue to Ste Apolline whose torturers pulled out all her teeth. She is now the patron saint of dentists. Although technically a market town, the description is rather an understatement, as St Pol is the number-one town in France for the cultivation of early vegetables, particularly artichokes, cauliflowers, potatoes, onions, carrots and flower bulbs, hence the nickname for the area of the 'Golden Band' (the Brittany Ferry in fact started its cross-Channel life as a carrier of vegetables, not people).

Carantec

Just across the estuary from Roscoff, this small family resort is very like a Cornish village, not least because of its curved, hilly roads, purpose-built to expand any driver's biceps. The town is centred around a superb expanse of golden beach where there is still plenty of picnicking room when the tide is in and where, as the sea recedes, a huge shallow pool is unveiled, usually packed with children. Here the buzz word is 'windsurf', the entire shallow bay being a mass of coloured sails during the summer, with the backdrop of cliffs echoing to the slap of sail on water and groans of exasperation.

Hôtel du Pors-Pol: it is like a treasure hunt trying to find this Logis hotel down the end of narrow, one-way lanes, but somehow the British *do* find it, many returning year after year to a world of respectable charm and calm. It is a large, solid, whitewashed building with arches painted on the walls above most of the ground-floor windows. It is popular with an older clientele, the majority of whom prefer to spend their days in the rose- and fuchsia-filled garden rather than confront the uphill struggle from the beach. The best accommodation bargain is the half-board, available only in September. (No street address: phone for directions.) ☎ 98 67 00 52. *Moderate.*

A Tour of the Enclosures

The Pays de Landi is the name of the area containing the best examples of Brittany's parish enclosures, churchyards with ornate, if crude, Calvaries and crosses. These structures, the product of the region's peace and prosperity of the fifteenth century, owe a great deal of their reputation to the burning desire of local masons and other craftsmen to express their faith in the symbolic language of carvings. The structures record in elaborate granite, wood and glass workmanship the alarming rivalry which dominated both the religious and municipal lives of the parish inhabitants. The following itinerary is designed to include a few of the more interesting Calvaries, ossuaries and arches, while absorbing some of the best of the Breton countryside on offer.

From Morlaix follow the main Paris–Brest route west, before turning south on the D785 to Plounéour-Ménez, famous for its bell tower, monumental triumphal arch and delightful houses clustered around the church Notre-Dame-du-Relecq. Roc'h Trévezel, a few kilometres further on, is the highest point in Brittany, 380 metres above sea level and worth climbing up to for spectacular views over endless horizons. At Commana there are two monuments worthy of a visit: the first is the Moulin de Kérouat, one of several old water mills once operating along the Elorn valley, now an open-air museum; the second is the famous Allée Couverte de Mougau-Vian where there is a communal Bronze Age tomb consisting of five slabs resting on sixteen supports, altogether some 14 metres long.

Follow the road north to the first of the well-known parish enclosures at the grey stone village of Saint-Thégonnec, whose ornate Calvary of mega proportions stands in the tiny cemetery there; it is the last of the large Breton Calvaries, and is made up of startlingly humorous caricatures. Continue to Guimiliau, whose church has an extraordinary sixteenth-century example with 200 human figures carved out of the granite to form tales from the Bible and Breton legends, and then to its counterpart Lampaul-Guimiliau, easily spotted by its unusually stunted spire – it was struck by lightning in the nineteenth century and was never rebuilt. The church has a magnificent baptistry, a moving Burial of

Christ, a remarkable six-faced pietà and other oak- and granite-carved works of art.

Return to Roscoff via a string of memorable places: Landivisiau, whose Kersanton-granite porch blends Gothic and Renaissance styles; Bodilis, whose magnificent sixteenth-century church has a flamboyant, Gothic spire, an unusual sculpted granite porch and carved furniture; St-Vougay and the nearby Château de Kerjean which is stuffed with old Breton furniture; and, finally, Berven. By winding up here you have the opportunity to examine the church's lantern-shaped dome and the arch leading to the parish close. You are also only 20 kilometres away from the Morlaix home base.

Auberge St Thégonnec: in case you get peckish en route, stop at this small but cosy little restaurant just down the road from the church at St Thégonnec. Marie-Thérèse and Alain Le Coz cook delicious salads, soufflés and fish dishes and are wonderfully friendly and welcoming. *Pl. de la Mairie,* ☎ *98 79 61 18. Inexpensive to moderate.*

St Malo

St Malo's fame is such that there are scores of people living in foreign countries who have not heard of Brittany but who have heard of St Malo. This reputation must be rooted in its maritime traditions, since its ships and sailors have long ago touched base in all parts of the globe. One of the most famous of its several famous sons, for example, was Jacques Cartier, who followed the course of the town's present cod fishermen to the banks off Newfoundland, discovered the St Lawrence estuary and thought he was in Asia. He was, of course, the first European to set foot in Canada.

St Malo is also the city of corsairs – a nest for legitimate pirates who were allowed to attack enemy ships, especially the British, at will in return for their booty. After nipping out to sea for their plunders they would then sail back through the reefs that surround the town and anchor in the river Rance under the protection of the city guns. But the town actually owes its name not to such heroic mariners but to a Welsh monk called Maclow, who, in the sixth century, became the Bishop of Alet, now the suburb of St Servan. What is now St Malo was then an uninhabited island in the estuary of the river Rance whose strategic value was later realised by the locals who took refuge there when invaded by the neighbouring Normans some ten centuries ago. Their fierce independence is a streak that runs throughout St Malo's history, a spirit reflected by the phrase 'I am neither a Frenchman nor a Breton but a Malouin.'

St Malo, as far as the tourist is concerned, means St Malo Intra-

Muros, the old town. It is a closely packed town bundled in behind medieval ramparts, its cobbled streets and ancient buildings just dying to be explored. But don't get too carried away by the apparent authenticity of these historic edifices. St Malo's grey granite and rather austere buildings may look old but look just a little closer and its history almost turns to yesterday. Some 80 per cent of the town was completely destroyed by American forces during the war; what you see today, for the most part, has been rebuilt in mostly eighteenth-century style as one of Europe's most shrewd and far-sighted reconstruction programmes.

Guy la Chambre, whose name has been bequeathed to the main square (though colloquially it is still called after another Malouin hero, the writer and one-time Ambassador to England François-René de Châteaubriand), is the man responsible for the town's post-war reconstruction. No matter what you may feel about St Malo's contrived antiquity, without his energy, and no doubt the long-term interests of tourism, St Malo would look like a Caen, Calais or Cherbourg. If the hordes of British, Germans, Scandinavians and Americans who linger in his square today, distracted by buskers and, it must be said, occasionally overcharged by the business interests, are not quite what he had in mind, the overall effect is stunning.

And just one word of warning. Beware St Malo's lethal seagulls – they've got it in for tourists and their cars and can overnight transform the blackest of limos into the whitest of carriages.

Do Not Miss

St Malo looks its most menacing from out at sea when an island of ramparts looms up beyond the maze of rocks and reefs like an impossible target of attack. Once the ferry has taken the harbour by storm and let you ashore, the best introduction to the town is to walk around its thirteenth- and fourteenth-century **ramparts**, touching history at every turn, most visibly in the form of statues of corsairs and explorers (some, no doubt, a key source of embarrassment to the more chauvinistic British visitors). Start at Porte St Vincent, or any of the other points of access, and just go round in circles. The variety of views is tremendous, especially from the watchtowers, with beaches to one side, ferries, ships and the Bassin Vauban yacht marina on the other; while across the bay busy with rocks, buoys and boats (including the fishermen off to Newfoundland in the wake of Cartier) you can see the popular resort of Dinard and the Emerald Coast beyond. You must do the walk twice, once at high tide and once at low. St Malo experiences the biggest tide in Europe so the view radically changes depending on the time of inspection. The range beween high and low can be as much as 14 metres and confidently floating yachts and fishing boats can be left abandoned in tiny puddles. The miniature town guide book must be one of the few in the world that contains tide tables for the year.

It is a surprise to find beneath the formidable backdrop of sheer walls a number of beaches, all clean though rather characterless strips. As the tide recedes, the sands grow in stature and personality, none more so than the main **Plage de Bon Secours** – as the sea recedes it reveals acres of sands, rockpools, a strip of causeway across to the **Ile du Grand Bé** (only accessible at low tide) and an entire swimming pool whose diving board seems at high tide just like the tip of an anonymous lump of concrete. For a broader expanse of beach, walk for fifteen minutes or catch a bus to the **Plage de Rochebonne**, a trip which can be conveniently combined with a visit to the nearby doll museum, the **Musée de la Poupée**, which is home to some 300 dolls in historic French costume, on the avenue Pasteur.

The **Historic Museum** is located in the Grand Donjon tower, great keep and gatehouses of the fifteenth-century **castle** in place Châteaubriand. Its exhibits show how thoroughly the old town was destroyed by the Americans while digging out Germans from within its walls in their push to join the British. There are also displays devoted to Châteaubriand and Jacques Cartier (we learned here that 'Canada' was the local Indian name for village) as well as lots of piratical paraphernalia – treasure chests, cannons, swords, peg legs and parrots as well as memorabilia of the town's two most famous corsairs, Robert Surcouf and René Duguay-Trouin. Also housed in the building is the **Quic-en-Groigne waxworks museum** with tableaux depicting the pirates of this historic city (forty-minute commentary tours in English are available during

the summer, leaving from the entrance every five minutes).
During the winter only the courtyard is open to visitors.

The **National Fort** was built by Vauban, Louis XIV's military
architect, in 1689, complete with ramparts, drawbridge and underground passage. During the siege of St Malo in 1944 the Germans
kept 380 hostages here. Located on the beach in front of the casino
and linked by a causeway at low tide, there are half-hour guided
tours available in English.

The **Aquarium** in place Vauban is really 100 aquariums built into
the walls of the ramparts and inhabited by 1000 specimens from
both the Channel and the Tropics. In the **Exotarium**, opposite the
Aquarium (entrance available on a combined ticket), you can see
some of the world's most peculiar reptiles. Open daily throughout
the year – from July to September it is open until 11 p.m.

Grand Bé island is accessible only via a causeway at low tide
(there are loudspeakers, whistles and a guard to herd visitors back
to the mainland as the tide turns). The island, which means 'tomb'
in Celtic, is where Châteaubriand chose to be buried beneath a
lonely granite cross, facing out to sea, left to relive his most famous
work, *Mémoires d'Outre-Tombe (Memories from Beyond the Grave)*.
From the top of the island there is a fantastic view of the entire
Emerald Coast.

Along with Paramé and Rotheneuf, **St Servan** was originally one
of three independent towns but is now blurred into greater St
Malo. All three are wise alternative places to stay if there is no room
in the Intra-Muros inns. Located just outside the St Malo ramparts,
separated by docks and locks, St Servan is really a resort in its own
right, with a famous fourteenth-century **Solidor Tower**, some 13
metres high, offering the best views of St Malo and the Rance
estuary and containing a museum devoted to ships that sailed
around Cape Horn.

Le Manoir de Jacques Cartier, the original home of the famous
Malouin who discovered Canada in 1534, is now a museum
devoted to his life and times. It is open during the summer from
Wednesday to Sunday only, in rue David Macdonald-Stewart in
Rotheneuf, another delightful seaside resort just beyond the walls
and famous for its sculptured rocks.

St Malo's **casino** is an impossible-to-miss building just outside the main Porte St Vincent. Inside, there are two discos and a restaurant for those with money left after visiting the gaming rooms. Open nightly in July and August, then weekends only, on the Esplanade du Casino (☎ 99 56 00 05).

Shopping Spree

Shopping in St Malo is sheer joy. The retailers here are more geared to the discerning needs of tourist traffic than in all the other ports. They cater less for the food buyer than, say, Boulogne or Calais do, with their far higher number of day-trip visitors, and more for people with money to spend on more exclusive items such as antiques and expensive clothes. But there's plenty tourist tat as well, from plastic crabs to 'been there, done that' badges (though most of these seem to be confined to rue de Dinan and rue St Vincent). The main shopping street threads more or less diagonally through the town from Porte St Vincent, changing its name as it goes. Most of the route is also pedestrian-only from lunchtime onwards during the summer.

Artdecor or **Maison Garel:** it seems to have two names but the result is the same; they – it – specialise in Breton lace with several designs based on the ancient Celtic triskele representing the three forces of nature: land, water and fire. The shop also sells fine lace gloves as well as embroidered cloth. *Rue de la Pie qui Boit (where it crosses rue Broussais).*

Arti: a fairly new shop selling Indonesian craft products including wooden bangles, marionettes from Bali, leather pouches and belts, earrings, unusually carved chess figures and carved wooden 'goblin bells'. *Rue de Pomme.*

Le Potier: sells the distinctive Grès sombre-shaded pottery from the centre of France, including interesting pitchers that have a special section for ice so that you can keep your white wine cool without diluting it. *Rue Jacques Cartier.*

La Boutique aux Fromages: its sign proclaims a specialist range of Swiss cheeses but in fact it carries an admirable range of French, neatly displayed on straw matting alongside tins of fancy biscuits.

They also sell butter, patted into shape with wooden bats just like they used to do in Sainsbury's umpteen years ago. *Rue de l'Orme.*

Au Poids du Roy: Mme Lessirard's neat, well-stocked and up-market *épicerie* is very popular with discriminating British shoppers, who come here for her stock of Bordeaux and Beaujolais wines originating from specific vineyards (particularly her supplies from a small Château Bouchard Aîné et Fils on the slopes of the Beaune). Madame also sells perfumed rice from Thailand, small pouches of wild rice from Canada, dried apricots, *flageolets verts, lingots, haricots rouges* and other more exotic pulses all displayed in baskets on an old pine table. As Mme Lessirard boasts, 'You can find many things here that you can't find there.' *Pl. du Poids-du-Roi.*

Maison de la Presse: standing on a key corner spot of town, this is the place to catch up with the latest English news, albeit a day or so later than the papers' publication, as well as a surprisingly diverse selection of magazines, from *The Economist* to *Rolling Stone*. It also stocks a good range of maps. *Corner of pl. du Pilori.*

Vertige: rather offhand staff who ignore you long enough for you to browse amongst their expensive and exceedingly elegant women's *prêt à porter* clothes without pressure. *Pl. du Pilori.*

Sport Mer: all the stock is pure Breton and *pur laine*: colourful pullovers and long coats, including duffels, in cream, red or blue, cardigans with navy badges, kids' clothes and Meralp red wool jackets. Labels include Le Minor, St-James, Armor, Tricomer and Busnel. *Pl. du Pilori.*

Aux Corsaires: a smart men and women's clothing store with every conceivable member of the colourful range of Lacoste shirts as the main attraction. *Pl. du Pilori.*

Francis Delouche: along with most of the other prettier European towns, antique shops flourish in St Malo. This is one of the most interesting, specialising in late nineteenth-century maritime articles such as boats in bottles, ships' wheels, brass compasses, lamps and telescopes and swashbuckling swords as well as scores of ornate canes, with handles serving a variety of non-walking functions (we saw a telescope, snuff box, watch, pen and ink, and a phial for booze, their prices often nudging £200 each). *Pl. Gasnier-Duparc.*

Cheftel: an elaborate, Regency-style pâtisserie with a *salon de thé* situated on a minstrels' gallery above. Try their *pavé de Pilo* made from almond, rum and crystallised fruits; *l'Ambre*, a nougat-flavoured chocolate mousse, or one of their unusual flavours of ice-cream. *Rue Porcon.*

Mahé Guilbert: sells chic Yves St Laurent, Daniel Hechter and Givenchy towelling dressing gowns in magnificent colours; the walls are hung with examples of their designer beach towels. *Rue Porcon.*

J. F. Busquet: the finest *charcuterie* in town, the shelves here are laden with pâtés, caviars, ciders, hams, gâteaux, salads and wines. *Rue Porcon.*

Faïencerie Malouine: the very friendly proprietor of this deceptively poky shop is almost hidden by stacks of Quimper-made *vaisselles de Bretagne*, plates, coffee bowls and other crockery typically bordered in blue and yellow and decorated with colourful figures, flowers and animals. The shop also makes and sells reproductions of famous antique designs. *Rue Porcon.*

Patates de Saint Malo: a cross between a shop and a stall that makes and sells *guinots* and *chiq' corsaire* humbug-shaped sweets (the latter on sticks – the St Malo equivalent of Kojak lollies), made on the premises according to an ancient Breton recipe and sold straight from the jar. *Rue Porcon.*

Spécimen and **Promod:** two neighbouring shops in St Malo's main shopping street, both sharing a high-tech stamp, bright colours and, it seemed, the same brand of loud vital music. The former sells trendy gear for *hommes*, the latter for *femmes. Rue St Vincent.*

La Sweaterie: just along the road you'll find a branch of the French chain, which, as its name suggests, stocks piles of brightly coloured sweatshirts. *Rue St Vincent.*

Monoprix: a comparatively small branch of the mega chain but the only grand store within the city walls selling all but the kitchen sink, including a wide range of groceries on the first floor. *Rue St Vincent.*

Bessec: a huge shoe shop with a wide range of nautical footware such as 'Aigle' sailing wellies and Docksides (real and mock versions), as well as cheap and cheerful canvas plimsolls, a rainbow selection of espadrilles and more standard ware. *Pl. de la Croix du Fief.*

La Cuisine Moderne: a modest range of Le Creuset, nests of red and white steaming pans and quality kitchen knives, but otherwise little of interest and rather offhand service. *Pl. de la Poissonnerie.*

Le Mazagram: the most interesting of its almost exclusively white Limoges porcelain range are tall, vase-shaped cups which were used by the French for coffee, mixed with eau-d'vie tipples, during their defence of Mazagram, Algeria, in 1840, when 124 French soldiers defended the town against thousands of Arabs. They can be upended and used as eggcups, and make an interesting variation on the souvenir theme. *Grande Rue.*

Le Tastevin: M. Robineau runs a minuscule shop hidden away in the corner of the Channel Isles' boat terminal with a selection of *propriétaire récoltant* and *viticulteur* wines, grown and bottled in small vineyards. His main business is in export to Jersey and sale to local restaurants but he is happy to sell to anyone. *Gare de la Bourse.*

Le Continent hypermarket stands on the south-western outskirts of the city. Take a number 6 bus from the railway station (departures are every fifteen minutes until 7.30 p.m., and tickets cost approx. 5 francs). Lots of car parking. *La Madeleine area.*

Every Tuesday and Friday morning there's a lively **market** in place du Marché aux Légumes. During the summer look for one particular stall, Au Petit Breton, run by Mme Lefort (who comes from Dinan and takes her stall to several other markets on different days of the week). She sells a huge range of blue and white striped Breton *pulls*, wool hats and other local knits, for significantly lower prices than the many other stores selling similar gear. Although the fruit and veg stalls operate all year, other summer-only stalls include clothing, basketry, and some of the cheese stalls.

Take a hint from the Malouins, who do the bulk of their food shopping in the huge covered market at the bottom of rue de l'Orme, on rue de la Herse, on Tuesday and Friday mornings. The rows of orderly stalls spill over with fresh produce: mushrooms from the Loire, fresh herbs and flowers, garlic, shallots, artichokes the size of World Cup footballs, bunches of radishes, chickens, quail, pigeons, ducks (not for the eyes of the squeamish, as they hang from their feet), strings of sausages, salamis, terrines of country pâtés, curd cheese and yogurt sold directly from churns and eggs in baskets. Plus a tiny pastry stall selling *galettes* and small trays of *Kouign Aman*, a buttered cake from Douarnenez, and the locally made *Breton aux pruneaux* cakes. A wonderful bustle.

A Place to Stay

With St Malo being such a year-round tourist honeypot, its hoteliers have long thrived in a sellers' market. Not only can it be hard to find a room during the peak of summer, but during the rest of the year you will pay rather more for a room here than in, say, neighbouring Roscoff or Cherbourg. St Malo tends to get especially packed to the ramparts in July and August, so, if you want to stay within the walls, reservations are essential. If you turn up on spec you will find accommodation but you'll almost certainly have to stay extra-muros.

Porte St-Pierre: a curious numbering of rooms (they descend as you climb the narrow, dimly lit steep stairs), plus the effort to get to the top, especially when armed with suitcases and unaided by any member of staff (we reckoned that you could almost live there for a few weeks before anyone took any notice of you) were rather an intimidating introduction to what turned out to be not a bad place to stay at all. Clean though poky rooms, comfy beds and really as much of France as you could find in any French hotel all compensate, as do the prices. So does the restaurant just across the road. Try the seafood platter – if there are two of you the portions could fill a dustbin lid (again, rotten service – at 10.30 p.m. while we were still eating they surrounded our island of intimacy with a forest of upturned chairs). *Pl. du Guet,* ☎ *99 40 91 27. Inexpensive to moderate.*

L'Univers: one of the few pre-war buildings in town that survived, luckily for the Germans who had chosen it for their place of residence. They had good taste, for the overall art nouveau style is magnificent, and we rate it as the best place to stay in St Malo. Although the bedrooms are fairly standard, the atmosphere of the downstairs foyer and rooms is highly seductive. The bar, which used to be the HQ of the St Malo yacht club, is a darkly wooded retreat whose walls are covered with fading pictures of yachts, old salts and charts. When dining, confront your huge, parchment menu and select your *entrées et frivolités* either in a conservatory full of plants or a high-ceilinged room decorated with chandeliers and Regency chairs. Breakfast is taken in yet another room surrounded by columns and murals. The lounge, decorated with international rotary club pennants, has a TV tuned into English channels, and pictures of the Queen reviewing the fleet at Spithead in 1953. As the *maitre d'* rightly says, 'British people will not be lost'. *Pl. Châteaubriand,* ☎ *99 40 89 52. Moderate.*

Hôtel Noguette: slap in the middle of town with an entire ground floor devoted to its restaurant, Mme Galpin's two-star establishment is as professionally run as many higher-graded places. *Rue de la Fosse,* ☎ *99 40 83 57. Moderate.*

La Pomme d'Or: well-positioned in the shadow of the walls where it has rested since 1585. A caged white pigeon, found wounded by the owners, greets new arrivals to the fifteen rooms. The restaurant has simple menus which offer, unusually, a choice of vegetables as a course. Not a stunningly friendly place but one that does its job conscientiously. *Pl. du Poids-du-Roi,* ☎ *99 40 90 24. Moderate to expensive.*

Quic-en-Groigne: full marks for the historic appearance of this building which is in fact just four years old; its foyer is decorated with maps of old St Malo in its pre-war days. A very peaceful, comfortable, unpretentious fifteen-roomed hotel, and by no means a kick in the groin (Quic-en-Groigne actually means 'complain as much as you like but we don't think you will want to'). Down the quiet *rue d'Estrées,* ☎ *99 40 86 81. Moderate.*

Aux Ajoncs d'Or: one of the few three-star hotels within the city walls, the Ajoncs d'Or has been completely refurbished to produce a light and airy foyer filled with plants, white cane furniture, a birdcage and a stuffed fox. Three floors, each with a characteristic flavour. We preferred the pine-clad attic rooms with Velux windows to the ubiquitous brown and yellow florid decoration elsewhere. High prices tend to attract more business clients than tourists according to Mme Laroche, who also refuses to put TVs in the rooms 'because there is far too much to see in St Malo'. *Rue des Forgeurs,* ☎ *99 40 85 03. Expensive.*

Le Valmarin: situated in St-Servan, this Relais du Silence mansion is shrouded by quiet surroundings and well deserves to belong to the 'chain of silence'. *Rue Jean XXII,* ☎ *99 81 94 76. Expensive.*

Central: affiliated to the Best Western chain, this large, popular hotel has forty-six largish rooms well tried and tested by British visitors. The restaurant looks like a railway carriage but the food is echelons above Travellers' Fare, especially if you go for the fish, its speciality. *Grande Rue,* ☎ *99 40 87 70. Moderate.*

And Somewhere to Eat

Like most regions of France, St Malo et environs reckons to have one of the leading gastronomies in the country. The seafood, particularly the crustaceans – crabs, mussels from the nearby Vivier beds (origin of some 25 per cent of the national intake), Cancale oysters and lobsters – as well as locally grown vegetables, notably artichoke and cauliflower, make the region famous for its fresh and healthy ingredients. This is also the place for pancakes, which may not sound too much of a gastronomic treat but their buckwheat flour base and toppings of anything from butter to sausage, egg and bacon to strawberry jam, are a meal unto themselves. They are, in other words, a different species to our bland Shrove Tuesday offerings. And if you are in particularly carnivorous mood you could opt for another local concoction, an authentic Châteaubriand, invented by the writer's chef: a grilled steak in a wine, shallot and tarragon sauce.

The rue de la Soif, named after the drunken sailors who once patronised the bars, and the area immediately surrounding Porte St Vincent is filled with restaurants that seem, more than any other

Channel port, totally geared up for the tourist. Each one has its own colour scheme like a resort, with matching canopies, tables and chairs to attract the strolling crowds. Since each tourist must pass this spot at least once during his or her stay, it is inevitably a prime spot.

Café de Paris: the traditional, Parisian-style meeting point in town, bang opposite Porte St Vincent. Lots of pavement tables and chairs where you can be served anything from a coffee to a meal by formal red waistcoated waiters. *Pl. Guy la Chambre*, ☎ *99 56 46 75. Inexpensive to expensive – it all depends on what takes your fancy.*

La Duchesse Anne: St Malo's queen of restaurants – a favourite lunchtime haunt of the expense-account businesspersons relishing lunch, and a mainly high-rolling tourist clientele at night. There is no fixed-price menu but the à la carte changes daily. Old-fashioned décor, cane chairs (half inside, half outside in the square under-neath a grand canopy), pink tablecloths, lace curtains, tiled floors, paddle fans and a menu that includes lobster at prices that won't send you scurrying for the next boat. But probably the one after that. Reservations essential. *Pl. Guy la Chambre*, ☎ *99 40 85 33. Moderate to expensive.*

Chantal: a crêperie offering the usual double menu of both savoury and sweet which you can watch being speedily made on large griddles behind the counter. There are more tables outside than in, and the former are often filled with school parties relishing the low, low prices and washing down the solids with naughty tipples of *cidre bouché. Pl. aux Herbes*, ☎ *99 40 93 97. Inexpensive.*

Louisiane: the exotic 'pirate' menu at this restaurant-cum-bar-cum-jazz club begins with a glass of punch and accras, followed by Antilles blood sausage, a fish of the day cooked in spices, creole style, and culminates in an *exotique coupé*. There are other imagina-tive menus, including more staid versions for the less adventurous. The bistroesque interior, with an Elton John-scale grand piano, dominates the dining room, and in the cellar a jazz quartet plays every evening from 10.30 p.m. to 4. a.m. *Rue des Cordiers*, ☎ *99 40 88 88. Moderate.*

Les Ecluses: chef M. Lempérière, who comes fresh from a string of Parisian restaurants, has one of the most innovative menus in town, which will perhaps come as a surprise considering its location in the Channel Islands' hydrofoil transport terminal. All his fish are steamed in seaweed-flavoured water and, as another example of M. Lempérière's individuality, the cheeseboard is wholly goat except for hot Meaux Brie served on toast with a nut salad. Good views overlooking the harbour and hydrofoil comings and goings. *Gare Maritime de la Bourse,* ☎ *99 56 81 00. Moderate to expensive.*

A l'Abordage: stands right in the heart of the fish market, so you won't be surprised to learn that this fish restaurant is one of the best in town, although the cramped seating, gilt-painted chairs and frilly lace tablecloths are just a little over the top for comfort. *Pl. de la Poissonnerie,* ☎ *99 40 87 53. Moderate.*

Le Chalut: a jaunty blue frontage announces this two-year-old restaurant, which comes highly recommended by several guides to good dining and rated the best by us. The interior furnishings are modern, like the owner, and mostly blue, decorated with fishing nets, lifebelts and other nautical niceties. The menu is almost exclusively devoted to fish, most of which make their first appearance either on a large stainless steel tray outside the restaurant or swimming about in a large tank inside the restaurant. Menus are chalked up on a blackboard in the window, and there's always a colossal *plateau des fruits de mer,* including half a lobster, and one of almost everything else that lives in a shell. *Rue Corne de Cerf,* ☎ *99 56 71 58. Inexpensive to moderate.*

Nuts and Bolts

The Brittany ferry terminal lies just outside the city walls, a few minutes' walk from the centre. On disembarkation just follow the Intra-Muros signs through the main gateway (St Vincent) and you will pick up signs indicating hotels. On your return journey don't cut your timing too fine – the roads to the ferry terminal slide back to let boats pass underneath, and even the smallest yacht will hold up the flow of traffic.

St Malo is also easily accessible from the Channel Isles. Several companies operate hydrofoil services to Jersey and Guernsey from the slick new conservatory-like terminal at Garé Maritime de la Bourse, and Emeraude Ferries operate a similar service from the Gare Maritime du Naye (☎ 99 82 41 41).

Guided walking tours of St Malo are available in July and August, each tour lasting 1½ hours at a cost of approximately 8 francs. Details from the tourist office at Port des Yachts (☎ 99 56 64 48).

Around and About

If you are going to spend your holiday in the wild and spacious Breton countryside or in hotter climes beyond, you can drive straight off the ferry and never pass within St Malo's ramparts. Though that, of course, would be a pity.

St Malo is an excellent gateway for exploring the Ille-et-Vilaine, a flat, marshy, richly agricultural area broken by forests and moorland, laced with several rivers and bordered to the south by the castles of the Loire Valley and to the north by the Emerald Coast. The area is named after the two principal rivers that cross it, the Ille and the Vilaine, which today, unlike during the region's commercial heyday, carry mainly holiday cruisers relishing the beauties of Brittany. Their confluence is in the region's capital, Rennes.

The Ille-et-Vilaine lacks many traditionally Breton aspects such as language and the folkloric festivals known as *pardons*, preferring to remain more typically French than Finistère to the west. Its unique characteristic is its mythological association with King Arthur and the Knights of the Round Table; more concrete elements of history are contained in the 300 or so Celtic megaliths – menhirs (symbols of eternity), dolmens and cairns – dotted around the landscape.

Dinard

Described both as the 'pearl of the Emerald coast' and the 'Nice of the north', and facing St Malo across the mouth of the River Rance, Dinard is Brittany's answer to fashionable Deauville or Le Touquet.

Its warm climate, enhanced by the Gulf Stream, has long been patronised by wealthy British who started renting holiday homes here in the 1850s, and it still retains its Belle Epoque charms, mostly in the shape of grand villas that you won't see anywhere else other than on the Côte d'Azur. Its three flat, sandy beaches are well sheltered and lapped by shallow, turquoise waters.

To trace the history of the town in detail, visit Villa Eugénie near the church (open daily, afternoons only, rue des Français Libres). However, the best way to soak up Dinard's airs is simply to take a walk along the exotic-palm-lined prom. Inland, the town has its full quota of swimming, fishing, golf, gambling, yachting and tennis facilities, and, if you decide to put its hospitality to the test, some excellent, old-fashioned hotels.

Grand Hôtel: if you can afford to do Dinard in the style to which it has become accustomed, stay here. Created by Americans and English for the use of Americans and English, St Malo has nothing to match it. Its restaurant is every bit as chic as you could imagine and so are the prices. *Av. George V,* ☎ *99 46 10 28. Expensive.*

Emeraude-Plage: a compromise on the Grand for those on a tighter budget, this is not a stretch of sand but a turn-of-the-century villa near the main beach, and its prices are roughly half those of the Grand. *Blvd Albert 1er,* ☎ *99 46 15 79. Moderate to expensive.*

Le Petit Robinson: a restaurant housed in an old villa just outside town with highly reputed nouvelle cuisine. *La Richardais,* ☎ *99 46 14 82. Moderate to expensive.*

Dinan

Just over the border of Ille-et-Vilaine, presiding over the picturesque Côtes-du-Nord region, is the magnificent town of Dinan. It lies across the river Rance, upstream from St Malo, and is a gem of historic buildings, all surrounded by three and a half kilometres of ramparts whose towers and gateways offer superb views over the lush river valley 60 metres below. An alternative place to just sit and stare in Dinan is in the shady Jardin Anglais, named after its visitors from Britain who have been coming to pay their respects for the last 150 years.

The best way to approach Dinan is on the water – boats leave first from St Malo and then pick up at Dinard. Their schedules depend on the tide; on certain days the trip isn't even a possibility, so check with the tourist office. Ideally, since the boat ride takes two and a half hours, you should leave early in the morning, have lunch and time to spare in Dinan and return in the afternoon. On Thursdays you'll catch Dinan's market, a sprawling, chaotic affair in the places du Champ and du Guesclin (the latter named after the town's hero, Bertrand du Guesclin, who defended it against the English in the Middle Ages); there's also a daily fish market in rue de la Chaux.

More adventurous travellers will no doubt prefer to make their way to Dinan by way of the Sentier de Grande Randonnée footpath, the GR 34, which adheres to the broad banks of the Rance where you can enjoy scenery that has been compared, perhaps with just a hint of exaggeration, to the Turkish Bosphorous. Taking this route, you'll pass the impressive *barrage*, the world's first tidal hydro-electric station, built to harness the river's powerful tides.

Hotel Marguerite: a Logis de France whose cheerful rooms are ceaselessly popular with British tourists, though those in need of silent nights should opt for a back room – the rooms in front have a view of the busy central place du Guesclin with Bertrand's equestrian statue. There's a beautifully decorated restaurant where in winter you can toast your cockles at an open fire and in all seasons taste some of the best local fish dishes. *Pl. du Guesclin*, ☎ *96 39 47 65. Inexpensive to moderate.*

La Caravelle: fourteen simple rooms, but far more impressive is the restaurant. Highly rated by Gault/Millau, chef Jean Claude Marmion's creations may prove just a shade too exotic for the staid British palate (skate salad with pears, brain tart with onions, pasta with chocolate sauce, for example). *Pl. Duclos*, ☎ *96 39 00 11. Expensive (hotel inexpensive).*

D'Avaugour: backed by gardens and ramparts and facing the statue of du Guesclin, this popular restaurant sometimes serves curried oysters and always fish. *Pl. du Guesclin*, ☎ *96 39 07 49. Moderate to expensive.*

Dol-de-Bretagne

Dol takes its name from the Breton word for table – Mont Dol, which rises from the surrounding marshlands to protect the town's northern frontier, is flat-topped. It is an attractive little town, strikingly medieval and situated on the border of Normandy and Brittany. Apart from its good looks, Dol is famous as producer of a large proportion of the *mouton de pré-salé* lamb, which is reared on Dol's salt pastures, and which features on several local menus.

Most of Dol's old houses cluster around the eleventh-century St Samson's cathedral. With its 100-metre nave and superb windows, it rates as one of the most beautiful in Brittany and would more than justify a Dol detour in its own right. For a bird's-eye view of town take a walk along the former moat fortifications, known as Les Douves. If your visit coincides with Saturday's market, the entire length of La Grande Rue, you'll need an additional couple of hours drifting along the rows of stalls. Just to the south-east of town, on the road towards La Boussac, stands Le Menhir du Champ Dolent, which, at 9 metres, is the highest free-standing megalith in Brittany.

Bretagne: a white-walled Logis near the cathedral, better rated for its rooms than its restaurant. *Pl. Châteaubriand,* ☎ *99 48 02 03. Inexpensive to moderate.*

Mont-Saint-Michel Bay

As Victor Hugo wrote, 'with her cathedral tiara and fortress armour, Mont-Saint-Michel is to the sea what Cheops is to the desert'. Perched high on a sudden outcrop of rock and reached by causeway across either a sea of sand or water, depending on the state of the massive tides, the medieval cathedral and former Benedictine abbey has been attracting pilgrims since the tenth century. Today's pilgrims come less for its spiritual, intellectual and artistic sanctuary but just to admire this unique structure which ranks as the second most visited monument in the country after Paris.

Mont-Saint-Michel's abbey was rescued from its status as a prison and made a national monument in 1874, whereas the actual

Mont has ranked amongst France's listed sites since only 1984. The town that clusters at the foot of the abbey comprises picturesque half-timbered houses, clinging to the side of the rock and lining the rue Principale. Some are museums that house armoury, paintings and sculptures from the Middle Ages as well as a collection of 250 old sailing vessels, and shops that originally sprang up to sell souvenirs to worshipping pilgrims and today still do, specialising in leather, pottery and faiences. The entire town is surrounded by high fortification walls and everything seems a steep climb away. The abbey, built and added to between the thirteenth and sixteenth centuries, is open daily (only 6000 at a time, please), as are the museums, between February and November. Boat trips to Mont-Saint-Michel leave St Malo (St Vincent pier) Monday to Saturday between July and September, 7.35 a.m. to 12.15 p.m. Alternatively, take a round trip organised by *courriers bretons*, which leaves St Vincent daily between 1 July and 15 September at 9 a.m., taking in Paramé, Rothéneuf, La Guimorais, Le Grouin, Cancale (famous for its oysters), Pontorson, Mont-Saint-Michel (free time here for five hours) and Dol, returning to St Malo at 6 p.m.

No Breton seafood plate would be complete without oysters or mussels from the Bay. Just off the coast at Le Vivier lie 450 hectares of oyster beds which produce more than 3000 tons of European and Portuguese oysters. Twice each day, as the tide drains out of Mont-Saint-Michel Bay, it reveals thousands of mussels clustering on wooden piles that would stretch for hundreds of miles if placed end to end.

The best way of discovering the hidden delights of the entire bay area is from the back of a 'mermaid'. An amphibious 150-passenger vehicle called La Sirène de la Baie (and nicknamed the Mermaid) leaves daily every two hours during the summer from Vivier-sur-Mer for a 1½ hour cruise/drive around mussel beds, Mont-Saint-Michel, Cancale, beaches and other highlights of these tidal expanses. On board you are served samples of seafoods in season and there are daily lunch cruises. Reservations: ☎ 99 46 82 30.

Le Bricourt: one of the most famous restaurants in Brittany, housed in an old manor house, whose two dining rooms would be acclaimed for their antiquities alone. Here you can dine from several menus – not all at once, though they all tend to kick off with the ubiquitous oysters. Michelin-starred nouvelle cuisine but with abundant helpings. *Rue du Guesclin, Cancale,* ☎ *99 89 64 76. Moderate.*

L'Armada: two sides of this modern restaurant are windowed to take advantage of its prime position at the end of the quay. The proprietor has a penchant for flower arranging, and there are as many filled vases on the tables and round the walls as he can manage and they can hold. Light and airy reflections from Mont-Saint-Michel fill the pale blue dining area, where scallops, lobster, *langoustines* and other fishy varieties are prepared by chef Nadine Perrigault who is a member of the prestigious Dames Cuisinières de France – a guarantee of the quality of the fish she serves. *Quai Thomas,* ☎ *99 89 60 02. Moderate.*

Restaurant des Parcs: a new restaurant situated near the church in Cherrueix. It has little by way of character but a lot by way of cuisine, thanks to the blend of classic and nouvelle styles offered by chef/owner M. Abraham, who used to own one of the best restaurants in Paimpol. Lots of fish dishes flavoured with herbs grown in his garden. *Cherrueix,* ☎ *99 48 82 26. Moderate.*

Combourg

Châteaubriand obviously had an eye for beauty – he spent most of his childhood in the pretty little lakeside town of Combourg, living in the family castle (which he believed was haunted by a black cat and a man with a wooden leg). The fifteenth-century building is in the town centre, its magnificent turrets visible for miles around. Just outside Combourg in Quebriac is a new museum, the Musée Internationale de la Faune, with more than 100 stuffed animals from all over the world, from the Arctic pack-ice to the African deserts, from the marshes of South America to the summits of the Himalayas. Open April to October only (rest of the year during national holidays only).

Du Château and **Du Lac:** two Logis de France hotels that face each other on opposite sides of the main square in the lee of Combourg castle are both recommended, the former particularly for its chef who cooks classic French cuisine, the latter for its tranquil location overlooking a lake that pops up from time to time in Châteaubriand's novels. *Du Château: pl. Châteaubriand, ☎ 99 73 00 38. Moderate; Du Lac: pl. Châteaubriand, ☎ 99 73 05 65. Inexpensive to moderate.*

Pleugueneuc

The Château de la Bourbansais at Pleugueneuc is Brittany's answer to Woburn Abbey. Inside the magnificent country house, which has belonged to the de Lorgeril family for 400 years, you can indulge vicariously in the life of the French aristocracy in a setting of antique furniture, paintings and other historical artefacts. Outside, 100 hectares have been transformed into a zoo, where tigers, monkeys, camels and flamingoes roam in a natural environment. Open daily in summer, every afternoon in spring and autumn.

The Forest of Paimpont

On the extreme western fringe of the Ille-et-Vilaine is the Brittany of King Arthur and his Knights of the Round Table, whose ghosts are still around to roam the spooky dells in search of the Holy Grail. Merlin lived here too, with Vivien the fairy. The 7000 hectares of forest, the most famous in Brittany, are all that remain of the forest of Brocéliande which, in the first century, covered the entire interior of the *département*. There are lots of waymarked paths through the forest (look hard and you may find Merlin's tomb) and fourteen lakes; there's also an excellent suggested itinerary for motorists that you can pick up from the Syndicat d'Initiative in Paimpont, the tourist hub town in the heart of the forest, with a huge, medieval abbey at the top of the main street.

Manoir du Tertre: a portrait of a previous owner, a fully-fledged Druid, hangs inside this one-star hotel, which has an excellent restaurant with a surprising repertoire and a few simple rooms (the character of the rooms has more to do with age than image). It sits alone on a hill just outside town, surrounded by beautiful landscaped gardens – you could almost imagine Mme Alix striving to create the perfect retreat for lovers. *Paimpont, ☎ 99 07 81 02. Moderate.*

Motoring Itinerary

If you want to link up all the above, the Route Châteaubriand (itinerary available from any tourist information centre in the region) covers Pleugueneuc, Combourg, Fougères, Vitre, Rennes (which is administratively but not aesthetically important), Moncontour, Cap Fréhel and Dinan. It has been devised to include some nineteen castles and monuments associated one way or another with the author Châteaubriand. In fact, having 'completed the course', you would have a knowledge of most of the area's heritage under your belt.

The route visits Fougères, which Victor Hugo described as the Carcassonne of the north, and its imposing, medieval castle which sits in an almost circular loop of the river Nançon skirted by well-laid-out gardens. With its thirteen towers strung out along its ramparts, it claims to be a unique remnant of Middle-Ages architecture. The fortified town of Vitre on the river Vilaine, has winding old streets and timbered houses with slate façades and a formidable triangular Château des Rochers, which played a significant role in the struggles between Britain and France and the defence of the vulnerable Pays des Marches de Bretagne.

Anyone whose appetite for castles is unsatiated by the Châteaubriand itinerary can branch off at Vitre and follow the *route touristique des Marches de Bretagne*, which links a number of châteaux on a magnificent route south beyond the Loire and Nantes. These were built to fortify the border and preserve the independence of Brittany from its two powerful and greedy neighbours, the Kingdom of France and the Plantagenet Duchy of Normandy.

Appendices

Cross Channel Ferries

Britain to France

From	To	Ferry Company	Crossing time (approx.)
Ramsgate	Dunkirk	Sally Line	2h30
Dover	Calais	Sealink/UK	1h30
Dover	Calais	Hoverspeed	35m
Dover	Calais	Townsend Thoresen	1h15
Dover	Boulogne	Townsend Thoresen	1h40
Dover	Boulogne	Hoverspeed	35m
Folkestone	Boulogne	Sealink/UK	1h50
Newhaven	Dieppe	Sealink Dieppe Ferries	4/5h
Portsmouth	Le Havre	Townsend Thoresen	5h30 (day) 8h (night)
Rosslare	Le Havre	Irish Continental Line	21h
Portsmouth	Caen	Brittany Ferries	5h30
Poole	Cherbourg	Brittany-Truckline	4h30
Portsmouth	Cherbourg	Sealink/UK	4h45
Portsmouth	Cherbourg	Townsend Thoresen	4h45
Weymouth	Cherbourg	Sealink/UK	4h15
Rosslare	Cherbourg	Irish Continental Line	18h
Portsmouth	St Malo	Brittany Ferries	8h30/10h
Plymouth	Roscoff	Brittany Ferries	6h30/7h
Cork	Roscoff	Brittany Ferries	19h

Source: British Tourist Authority

Ferry Company Offices and Reservations

Sealink UK Ltd
Southern House
Lord Warden Square
Dover
Kent CT17 8DH
(☎ 0304 203203)

Sealink UK Ltd
Newhaven Harbour
Newhaven
East Sussex BN9 0BG
(☎ 0273 514131)

Sealink UK Ltd
Norman House
Kettering Terrace
Portsmouth
Hampshire PO2 7AE
(☎ 0705 811315)

Sealink UK Ltd
Weymouth Quay
Weymouth
Dorset DT4 8DY
(☎ 0305 786363)

Sealink UK Ltd
Car Ferry Terminal
Folkestone Harbour
Kent CT20 1QH
(☎ 0303 53949)

Townsend Thoresen
Enterprise House
Channel View Road
Dover
Kent CT17 9TJ
(☎ 0304 214422)

Townsend Thoresen
Continental Car Ferry Port
Mile End

Portsmouth
Hampshire
(☎ 0705 827677)

Sally Line Ltd
54 Harbour Parade
Ramsgate
Kent CT11 8LN
(☎ 0843 595522)

Brittany Ferries UK Ltd
Millbay Docks
Plymouth
Devon PL1 3EW
(☎ 0752 221321)

Brittany Ferries UK Ltd
The Brittany Centre
Wharf Road
Portsmouth
Hampshire PO2 8RU
(☎ 0705 827701)

Hoverspeed Ltd
International Hoverport
Ramsgate
Kent CT12 5HS
(☎ 0843 54881)

Brittany Ferries UK Ltd
Tourist House
542 Grand Parade
Cork
Eire
(☎ 021 507666)

Irish Continental
Line
19 Aston Quay
Dublin 2
Eire
(☎ 01 775693)

Motoring Organisations, including Offices at Ports of Entry

The various motoring organisations, several of which have offices at ports of entry, have a fund of expertise that can be consulted. Membership of your corresponding national motoring organisation can provide you with use of either AA, RAC or RIAC facilities – to find out about such reciprocal arrangements consult your own motoring organisation or apply to:

The Automobile Association
Fanum House
Basingstoke
Hampshire RG21 2EA
☎ Basingstoke (0256) 20123

The Royal Automobile Club
RAC House
PO Box 100
Landsdowne Road
Croydon CR9 2JA
☎ 01–686 2525

RAC Port Service Centres

Dover
RAC Port Office
Terminal Building
Eastern Docks
Dover Harbour
☎ Dover (0304) 204256 and
204153

Folkestone
RAC Port Office
West Side Terminal
Folkestone Harbour
☎ Folkestone (0303) 58560

Guernsey
RAC Port Office
St Julian's Pier
St Peter Port
☎ Guernsey (0481) 20822

Harwich
RAC Port Office
Parkeston Quay
☎ Harwich (0255) 503567

London
Michael Gibbons & Co Ltd
6 Dock Street
☎ 01–480 5011

Ramsgate
RAC Port Office
Military Road
☎ Thanet (0843) 588452

Newhaven
RAC Port Office
Ferry Terminal

Newhaven Harbour
☎ Newhaven (0273) 514068

Portsmouth
RAC Port Office
Rudmore Roundabout
☎ Portsmouth (0705) 697713

Southampton
RAC Port Office
Car Park
West Quay Road
☎ Southampton (0703) 24244

AA Port Service Centres in Britain

Dover
Eastern Dock Terminal
☎ Dover (0304) 208122
Snargate Street
☎ Dover (0304) 206780

Folkestone
Folkestone Harbour
☎ Folkestone (0303) 58111

Guernsey
The White Rock
St Peter Port
☎ Guernsey (0481) 22984

Harwich
Car Ferry Terminal
Parkeston Quay
☎ Harwich (0255) 50331

Newhaven
Car Ferry Terminal
Newhaven Harbour
☎ Newhaven (0273) 514245

Plymouth
Millbay Docks
☎ Plymouth (0752) 665437

Portsmouth
Wharf Road
Rudmore Roundabout
☎ Portsmouth (0705) 698854

Ramsgate
International Hoverport
Pegwell Bay
☎ Thanet (0843) 52940

Southampton
No. 2 Gate, Eastern Docks
Southampton
☎ Southampton (0703) 28304

Weymouth
Weymouth Quay
☎ Weymouth (0305) 786057

DUTY AND TAX FREE ALLOWANCES

1. CUSTOMS DECLARATION

Each person in your vehicle should read this notice and tell you whether they have anything to declare to Customs. You should then display the appropriate red or green sticker.

Vehicles are part of an importer's belongings. Those with RED stickers will be directed to the Customs Officer. Those with GREEN stickers will normally be allowed to proceed after a brief stop, but the Customs Officer may decide upon a more detailed examination of the vehicle and its contents. UK residents may be required to satisfy the Customs Officer that their vehicles have already borne duty and/or VAT and car tax.

2. VISITORS

If you are a visitor to the United Kingdom you may generally bring in all your personal belongings in your luggage free of duty and tax. However, for tobacco products, alcoholic drinks, perfume and toilet water, you are restricted to the allowances shown at 4 below. All your personal belongings must be taken with you when you leave the UK.

3. PROHIBITED AND RESTRICTED GOODS

IMPORT CONTROLS. The Customs Officer will be able to provide full information. This is a list of the commoner and more frequently met items:–

- Controlled drugs, such as opium, heroin, morphine, cocaine, cannabis, amphetamines and lysergide (LSD).
- Firearms, (including gas pistols, electric shock batons, similar weapons and imitation firearms), ammunition and explosives (including fireworks).
- Flick knives.
- Counterfeit currency.
- Horror comics. Indecent or obscene books, magazines, films, video cassettes and other articles.
- Radio transmitters, (Walkie-Talkies, Citizen's Band radios etc), not approved for use in the UK.
- Meat and poultry, and most of their products (whether or not cooked) including ham, bacon, sausage, pâté, eggs and milk.
- Plants and plant produce, such as fruit, vegetables, bulbs and seeds.
- Most animals and birds, whether alive or dead (eg stuffed); certain articles derived from protected species including furskins, ivory, reptile leather and goods made from them. NOTE cats, dogs and other mammals must not be landed unless a British import licence (rabies) has previously been issued.

EXPORT CONTROLS. The following are some of the goods subject to export controls and should be declared to the Customs Officer. There are formalities to be completed in respect of these goods prior to your arrival at the port of exportation and further information is available through any local office of Customs and Excise (address in the phone book) – but not our VAT offices.

- Controlled drugs.
- Firearms and ammunition.
- Photographic material over 60 years old and valued at £200 or more.
- Portraits (including sculptures) of British historical personages which are over 50 years old and valued at £2000 or more.
- Antiques, collectors' items etc (including paintings and other works of art) over 50 years old and valued at £8000 or more.
- Certain archaeological material.
- Most live animals and birds, and items made from animals occurring wild in the U.K.

4. DUTY AND TAX FREE ALLOWANCES

Column 1 Goods obtained duty and tax free in the EC, or duty and tax free on a ship or aircraft, or goods obtained outside the EC.		Column 2 Goods obtained duty and tax paid in the EC.
Tobacco products		**Tobacco products**
200 cigarettes or 100 cigarillos or 50 cigars or 250 grammes of tobacco ⎫ double if you live outside Europe	or	300 cigarettes or 150 cigarillos or 75 cigars or 400 grammes of tobacco
Alcoholic drinks		**Alcoholic drinks**
2 litres of still table wine	or	5 litres of still table wine
plus		**plus**
1 litre over 22% vol. (eg. spirits and strong liqueurs) or 2 litres not over 22% vol. (eg low strength liqueurs or fortified wines or sparkling wines) or a further 2 litres of still table wine	or	1½ litres over 22% vol. (eg. spirits and strong liqueurs) or 3 litres not over 22% vol. (eg low strength liqueurs or fortified wines or sparkling wines) or a further 2 litres of still table wine

Persons under 17 are not entitled to tobacco and drinks allowances.

Perfume		**Perfume**
50 grammes (60 cc or 2 fl oz)	or	75 grammes (90 cc or 3 fl oz)
Toilet water		**Toilet water**
250 cc (9 fl oz)	or	375 cc (13 fl oz)
Other goods		**Other goods**

£28 worth, but no more than:—
   50 litres of beer
   25 mechanical lighters
	or	£207 worth, but no more than:—
		   50 litres of beer
		   25 mechanical lighters

5. Notes on the allowances

1. You are entitled to either column 1 or column 2, *but not both,* for each category of goods, (each category being defined by a red box).
2. You cannot get the higher allowances by mixing goods obtained duty & tax-free or outside the EC with goods obtained duty & tax-paid in the EC e.g. you cannot import 200 cigarettes from a duty-free shop with 100 cigarettes obtained duty & tax-paid in the EC, to get the 300 (column 2 category) cigarettes allowance.
3. You can however mix "duty-free" spirits and liqueurs with "duty-paid" still table wine, as these are in separate categories under the alcoholic drinks allowance. Exceptionally if you take the further allowance of still table wine in place of spirits etc, you may mix such wine obtained "duty-free" even if the main allowance (5 litres) has been obtained "duty-paid".
4. Whisky, gin, rum, brandy, vodka and most liqueurs normally exceed 22% vol. but aperitifs may be less.
5. The countries of the EC (Common Market) are Belgium, Denmark, France, West Germany, Greece, the Irish Republic, Italy, Luxembourg, the Netherlands, Portugal, Spain (but not the Canary Islands) and the United Kingdom (but not the Channel Islands).
6. The responsibility for opening, unpacking and repacking your luggage rests with you.
7. Alcoholic drinks, tobacco products, perfume and toilet water are charged according to quantity and kind. Customs charges are likely to be substantially more than the price you paid.

Sizes/Weights and Measures

Sizes: Equivalences

SHOES
Chaussures

France	England
37	4
38	5
39	6
40	7
41	8
42	9
43	10

LADIES WEAR
Confection Dames

France	England
34n–36n	8
36n–38n	10
38n–40n	12
42n	14
44n	16
48n	18
50n	20

SOCKS
Chaussettes

France	England
39–40	9½
40–41	10
41–42	10½
42–43	11
43–44	11½

MENSWEAR
Confection Hommes

France	England
42	36
44	38
46	40
50	42
52	44
54	46

HATS
Chapeaux

France	England
54	6⅜
55	6¾
56	6⅞
57	7
58	7⅛
59	7¼

SHIRTS
Chemises

France	England
36	14
37	14½
38	15
39	15½
40	15¾
41	16
42	16½
43	17
44	17½

Weights and Measures: Equivalences

WEIGHT

100 grams	3.527 oz
1 kilo	2.205 lb
10 kilos	0.882 quarter
1 tonne	1.102 short ton

SURFACE

1 m²	1.197 sq. yard
1 km²	0.386 sq. mile
1 hectare (ha)	2.47 acres

LENGTH

1 millimetre (mm)	0.039 inch
1 centimetre (cm)	0.033 foot
1 metre (m)	1.094 yard
1 kilometre (km)	0.621 mile

VOLUME

1 cm³	0.064 cu. inch
1 dm³ (1 litre)	0.036 cu. foot
1 m³	1.309 cu. yard

LIQUIDS

1 litre	8.454 gills
1 litre	2.113 pints
1 litre	1.057 quart
1 litre	0.264 gallon